WILLIAM URY

GETTING TO

YES

WITH YOURSELF
(& OTHER WORTHY OPPONENTS)

Thorsons

To my teachers—
with profound gratitude

ALSO BY WILLIAM URY

Getting to Yes

Beyond the Hotline

Getting Disputes Resolved

Windows of Opportunity

Getting Past No

Getting to Peace
(published in paperback as
The Third Side)

Must We Fight?

The Power of a Positive No

HarperThorsons
An imprint of HarperCollins*Publishers*
1 London Bridge Street
London SE1 9GF

www.harpercollins.co.uk

First published in the US by HarperOne 2015
Published in Great Britain by HarperThorsons 2015

1 3 5 7 9 10 8 6 4 2

A catalogue record of this book is available from the British Library

ISBN 978-0-00-810605-8

Printed and bound in Great Britain by Clays Ltd, St Ives plc

MIX
Paper from
responsible sources

FSC www.fsc.org   **FSC™ C007454**

CONTENTS

THE FIRST NEGOTIATION

Let him who would move the world first move himself.

—SOCRATES

How can we get to *yes* with others? How can we resolve the conflicts that naturally arise with colleagues and bosses, spouses and partners, clients and customers, children and family members, indeed almost everyone we interact with? How can we get what we *really* want and at the same time deal with the needs of others in our lives? Perhaps no human dilemma is more pervasive or challenging.

I have been working on this dilemma throughout my professional life. Three and a half decades ago I had the privilege of coauthoring with my late mentor and colleague Roger Fisher *Getting to Yes: Negotiating Agreement Without Giving In*. That book helped people change the way they negotiate with others at work, at home, and in the community. With millions of copies in circulation around the world, it helped transform the popular mindset for dealing with differences from "win-lose" thinking to a "win-win" or "mutual gains" approach.

Reaching mutually satisfying agreements can often be highly challenging, however. Since the publication of *Getting to Yes,* I have had the opportunity to train tens of thousands of people in all walks of life in the methods of mutual gains negotiation: managers, lawyers, factory workers, coal miners, schoolteachers, diplomats, peacekeepers, parliamentarians, and government officials. Many report success in changing the game from "win-lose" to "win-win," but others struggle. Even if they have learned the basics of a win-win approach to negotiation, when placed in situations of conflict, they revert back to costly and destructive win-lose methods, usually attributing this reversion to the necessity of dealing with difficult people.

Because I have focused in my work on how to deal with difficult people and challenging situations, I thought I might be able to help further. So I wrote a follow-up book called *Getting Past No* and, in more recent years, another book called *The Power of a Positive No*. The methods described in these books have also helped many people to resolve their daily conflicts, but still I sensed something missing.

What was missing, I have come to realize, was the first and most important negotiation we ever conduct—the negotiation with ourselves.

Getting to yes with yourself prepares the way for getting to yes with others. I have come to think of this book as the missing first half of *Getting to Yes*. It is the necessary prequel, but thirty years ago I did not fully realize just how necessary. If *Getting to Yes* is about changing the outer game of negotiation, *Getting to Yes with Yourself* is about changing the inner game so that we can then change the outer game. After all, how can we really expect to get to yes with others, particularly in challenging situations, if we haven't first gotten to yes with ourselves?

OUR WORTHIEST OPPONENT

Whether we think of it or not, each of us negotiates every day. In the broad sense of the term, negotiation simply means the act of back-and-forth communication trying to reach agreement with others. Over the years, I have asked hundreds of audiences the question "Who do you negotiate with in the course of your day?" The answers I receive usually start with "my spouse or partner" and "my children," continue on to "my boss," "my colleagues," and "my clients," and finally to "everyone in my life all the time." But, every so often, one person will answer: "I negotiate with myself." And the audience inevitably laughs—with the laughter of recognition.

The reason why we negotiate is, of course, not just to reach agreement but to get what we want. Gradually, over the decades of mediating in a variety of difficult conflicts, from family feuds and boardroom battles to labor strikes and civil wars, I have come to the conclusion that the greatest obstacle to getting what we really want in life is not the other party, as difficult as he or she can be. The biggest obstacle is actually ourselves. We get in our own way. As President Theodore Roosevelt once colorfully observed, "If you could kick the person in the pants responsible for most of your trouble, you wouldn't sit for a month."

We sabotage ourselves by reacting in ways that do not serve our true interests. In a business dispute, one partner calls the other a liar in the press, shaming the other, who launches a lawsuit that is highly costly for both. In a sensitive divorce conversation, the husband loses his temper, lashes out at his wife, and storms out, undermining his own expressed interest in resolving the issue amicably for the sake of the family.

Underlying our poor reactions in moments of conflict is an adversarial "win-lose" mindset, the assumption that *either* we can get what we want *or* they can—but not both. Whether it is business titans struggling for control over a commercial empire or children fighting over a toy or ethnic groups quarreling over territory, the unspoken premise is that the only way one side can win is if the other loses. Even if we want to cooperate, we are afraid that the other person will take advantage of us. What sustains this "win-lose" mindset is a sense of scarcity, the fear that there is just not enough to go around, so we need to look out for ourselves even at the expense of others. All too often, the result of such "win-lose" thinking is that all sides lose.

But the biggest obstacle to our success can also become our biggest opportunity. If we can learn to influence ourselves first before we seek to influence others, we will be better able to satisfy our needs as well as to satisfy the needs of others. Instead of being our own worst opponents, we can become our own best allies. The process of turning ourselves from opponents into allies is what I call getting to yes with yourself.

SIX CHALLENGING STEPS

I have spent many years studying the process of getting to yes with yourself, drawing deeply on my personal and professional experiences as well as observing the experiences of others. I have tried to understand what blocks us from getting what we really want and what can help us satisfy our needs *and* get to yes with others. I have codified what I have learned into a method with six steps, each of which addresses a specific internal challenge.

The six steps may at times seem like common sense. But in my three and a half decades of working as a mediator, I've learned that they are *un*common sense—common sense that is *uncommonly* applied. You might be familiar with some or all of these steps individually, but my hope is to bring them together into an integrated method that will help you keep them in mind and apply them in a consistent and effective way.

In brief, the six steps are as follows:

1. **Put Yourself in *Your* Shoes.** The first step is to understand your worthiest opponent, yourself. It is all too common to fall into the trap of continually judging yourself. The challenge instead is to do the opposite and listen

empathetically for underlying needs, just as you would with a valued partner or client.

2. **Develop Your Inner BATNA.** Almost all of us find it difficult not to blame others with whom we come into conflict. The challenge is to do the opposite and to take responsibility for your life and relationships. More specifically, it is to develop your inner BATNA (*Best Alternative To a Negotiated Agreement*), to make a commitment to yourself to take care of your needs independently of what the other does or does not do.

3. **Reframe Your Picture.** A natural fear of scarcity exists in almost everyone. The challenge is to change how you see your life, creating your own independent and sufficient source of contentment. It is to see life as being on your side even when it seems unfriendly.

4. **Stay in the Zone.** It is so easy in the midst of conflict to get lost in resentment about the past or in anxieties about the future. The challenge is to do the opposite and stay in the present moment, the only place where you have the power to experience true satisfaction as well as to change the situation for the better.

5. **Respect Them Even If.** It is tempting to meet rejection with rejection, personal attack with personal attack, exclusion with exclusion. The challenge is to surprise others with respect and inclusion *even if* they are difficult.

6. **Give and Receive.** It is all too easy, especially when resources seem scarce, to fall into the win-lose trap and to focus on meeting only your needs. The final challenge is to change the game to a win-win-win approach by giving first instead of taking.

I have come to understand the process of getting to yes with yourself as a circular journey to an "inner yes," as the diagram depicts. This inner yes is an unconditionally constructive attitude of acceptance and respect—first toward yourself, then toward life, and finally toward others. You say *yes to self* by putting yourself in your shoes and developing your inner BATNA. You say *yes to life* by reframing your picture and staying in the zone. You say *yes to others* by respecting them and by giving and receiving. Each yes makes the next easier. Together these three yeses form a single inner yes that makes it considerably easier to reach agreement with others, particularly in challenging situations.

The Inner Yes Method

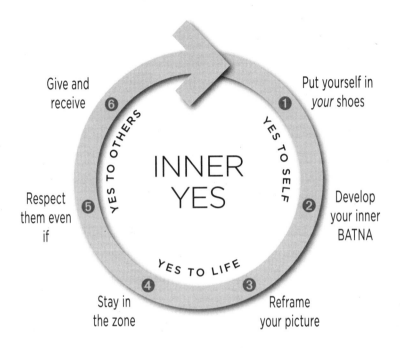

To help illustrate the inner yes method, I will draw on my own experiences as well as those of others. As a mediator and negotiation adviser in some of the toughest conflicts on the planet, I have had to train myself over the years to hold steady under pressure while being attacked by presidents and guerrilla commanders, to observe myself and suspend my reactions, and to respect people who are difficult to respect.

As I have found, the very same negotiating principles that

are used for getting to yes outside can be used for getting to yes inside. What works in resolving external conflict can work in dealing with internal conflict. If you have read my earlier books, you will find much of my vocabulary familiar but applied in an entirely different way, looking inward rather than outward. If you are not already familiar with my work, don't worry. I will explain enough so that this book stands on its own.

While getting to yes with yourself may sometimes seem simple, it is often far from easy. In fact, based on my personal and professional experience, I would say that the process of getting to an inner yes is some of the hardest work we ever have to do. We human beings, after all, are reaction machines. It is only natural to judge ourselves, to blame others, to fear scarcity, and to reject when rejected. As straightforward as listening to yourself, taking responsibility for your needs, or respecting others may appear, *doing* these things eludes us more than we would perhaps like to admit—and never more so than when we are in a conflict. I have tried to distill the process of getting to yes with yourself into its simplest form so that it will be easier to apply when the work gets tough and especially when emotions are running high.

Whatever difficulties may arise, however, the truth is that we are more than capable of overcoming them. The very best instrument we have for getting what we really want in life is in our hands. Through learning and practice, through examining our existing attitudes and testing out new ones, we can achieve results in personal satisfaction and negotiation success that are worth far more than the investment in time and effort. As I have personally experienced, getting to yes with yourself is not just the most challenging, but the most rewarding negotiation of all.

HOW TO USE THIS BOOK

You can use the inner yes method in a number of ways. One is to review the six steps *before* an important conversation or negotiation—ideally a day in advance to fully prepare, but in just a few minutes if you are in a jam. Reviewing the six steps will help ensure that you do not show up as your worst opponent, but rather as your best ally, when you interact with the other person. As you read this book, in fact, I encourage you to keep in mind a challenging situation or problematic relationship in your life. You will not only learn more and derive more benefit from your reading by applying the six steps to a specific situation, but you will also emerge better prepared to reach a mutually satisfying agreement with the other side.

Of course it will be a lot easier to get to yes with yourself in preparation for an actual negotiation if you have practiced the six steps regularly beforehand. Just as athletes train consistently in order to perform their best in a competition, so can you. Getting to yes with yourself is a daily practice, not just reserved for special situations. Every single day, we have multiple opportunities to listen for our underlying needs, to take responsibility for meeting those needs, and to change our stance from win-lose to win-win. In this way, we can head off unnecessary conflict and make our daily negotiations far easier. For those who are unaccustomed to looking inside themselves, the internal homework may feel like a bit of a stretch. It's okay to take it slow. As a lifelong hiker and mountain climber, I am a strong believer in taking long journeys in small steps.

Ultimately, the inner yes method offers a way of living your life and conducting your relationships with anyone, at home, at work, and in the world. Many readers may remember the insightful and useful book *The 7 Habits of Highly Effective People* by my late friend Stephen Covey. Like *The 7 Habits, Getting to Yes with Yourself* aims to offer you a set of life skills, a successful and satisfying way to live and work well with others that comes from learning to live and work well with yourself.

While *Getting to Yes with Yourself* seeks to improve your

ability to negotiate effectively, it is designed with a much broader goal in mind: to help you achieve the inner satisfaction that will, in turn, make your life better, your relationships healthier, your family happier, your work more productive, and the world more peaceful. My hope is that reading this book will help you succeed at the most important game of all, the game of life.

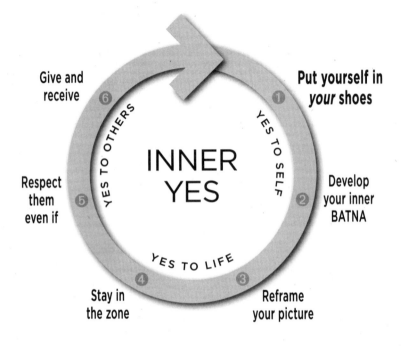

PUT YOURSELF IN *YOUR* SHOES

FROM SELF-JUDGMENT TO SELF-UNDERSTANDING

Know thyself? If I knew myself, I'd run away.

—JOHANN WOLFGANG VON GOETHE

While I was writing this book, I was approached for help by the wife and daughter of Abilio Diniz, a highly successful and prominent businessman from Brazil. Abilio was involved in a complex and protracted dispute with his French business partner, fighting over control of Brazil's leading supermarket retailer, a company that Abilio and his father had built up from a single bakery. While Abilio had sold controlling shares to the French, he remained as chair and major shareholder. A partnership that had started well years earlier had turned bitter. Two major international arbitration cases were in process as was a big lawsuit. The battle was the subject of constant speculation in the media. Who was winning? The *Financial Times* called the dispute "one of the biggest cross-continental boardroom showdowns in history."

Trapped in a conflict from which he could see no way out—a fight that consumed his time and resources—Abilio felt angry and frustrated. The general expectation was that the fierce battle, which had lasted for two and a half years, would go on for another eight years, by which point he would be well into his eighties.

After studying the case carefully, I had a chance to talk extensively with Abilio and his family at his home in São Paulo. As complicated and difficult as the conflict with the French partner seemed, I sensed that the first and fundamental obstacle lay within Abilio himself. A man of dignity, he felt very disrespected and ill-treated by his business partner. He did not know what he really wanted most, to fight or to settle. In and out of the boardroom, he often found himself reacting out of anger in ways that went contrary to his interests. Like most of us, he was his own worthiest opponent.

The first step in resolving the dispute, it seemed to me,

was for Abilio to figure out his true priorities. So I asked him, "What do you *really* want?" His first response was to give me a list: he wanted to sell his stock at a certain price; he wanted the elimination of a three-year noncompete clause that prevented him from acquiring other supermarket companies; and he wanted a number of other items including real estate. I pressed him again. "I understand you want these concrete items. But what will these things give you, a man who seems to have everything? What do you *most* want right now in your life?" He paused for a moment, looked away, then turned back to me and said with a sigh: "Freedom. I want my freedom." "And what does freedom give you?" I asked. "Time with my family, which is the most important thing in my life," he replied. "And freedom to pursue my business dreams."

Freedom then was his deepest need. Freedom is important to all of us but it had special resonance for Abilio because of a harrowing experience in his past. Years earlier, while leaving his home, he had been kidnapped by a band of urban guerrillas. Confined in a tiny cubicle with two pin-size holes for air and assaulted by intensely loud music, Abilio thought he would be killed at any moment. Fortunately, he was rescued in a surprise police raid after a week in captivity.

Once Abilio and I had clarity on his deepest need, freedom became the "north star" for our work together, orienting all our actions. When my colleague David Lax and I were able to sit down to negotiate with the other side, we were able to resolve within just four days this bitter and protracted dispute that had gone on for years. The solution was surprisingly satisfying for everyone, as I will recount later in this book.

We all wish to get what we want in life. But the problem is that, like Abilio, what we *really* want is often not clear to us. We may want to satisfy others in our lives too: our spouse or partner, colleagues, clients, even our negotiating opponents. But the problem is that what *they* really want is also often not clear to us.

When people ask me what is the most important skill for a negotiator, I usually respond that, if I had to pick just one, it would be the ability to put yourself in the other person's shoes. Negotiation, after all, is an exercise in influence, in trying to change someone else's mind. The first step in changing someone's mind is to know where that mind is. It can be very difficult, however, to put ourselves in the other person's shoes, particularly in a conflict or negotiation. We tend to be so focused on our own problems and on what *we* want that we have little or no mental space to devote to the other side's problem and what *they* want. If we are asking our boss for a raise, for instance, we may be so preoccupied with solving our problem that we don't focus on the boss's problem, the tight budget. Yet unless we can help the boss solve that problem, the boss is unlikely to be able to offer us a raise.

There is one key prior move, often overlooked, that can help us clarify both what we want and, indirectly, what the other person wants. That move is to put yourself in *your own* shoes first. Listening to yourself can reveal what you really want. At the same time, it can clear your mind so that you have mental and emotional space to be able to listen to the other person and understand what he or she really wants. In the example of the raise, hearing yourself out first can help you listen to your boss and understand the problem of the tight budget.

Putting yourself in *your* shoes may sound odd at first because, after all, are you not already in your own shoes? But to do it properly is not nearly as easy as it might appear. Our natural tendency is to judge ourselves critically and to ignore or reject parts of ourselves. If we look too closely, we may feel, as Goethe says, like running away. How many of us can honestly say that we have plumbed the depths of our minds and hearts? How many of us regularly listen to ourselves with empathy and understanding—in the supportive way that a trusted friend can?

Three actions can help. First, see yourself from the

"balcony." Second, go deeper and listen with empathy to your underlying feelings for what they are really telling you. Third, go even deeper and uncover your underlying needs.

SEE YOURSELF FROM THE BALCONY

Benjamin Franklin, known as a highly practical and scientific man, reflected in *Poor Richard's Almanack* more than two and a half centuries ago, "There are three things extremely hard: steel, a diamond, and to know one's self." His advice was: "Observe all men; thyself most."

If you observe yourself and others in moments of stress during negotiation and conflict, you will notice how easily people become triggered by the other person's words, tone of voice, and actions. In virtually every dispute I have ever mediated—whether it is a marital spat, an argument in the office, or a civil war—the pattern is reaction followed by reaction followed by yet another reaction. "Why did you attack him?" "Because he attacked me." And on it goes.

When we react, we typically fall into what I call the "3A trap": we *attack*, we *accommodate* (in other words, give in), or we *avoid* altogether, which often only makes the problem grow. Or we use a combination of all three approaches. We may start off avoiding or accommodating, but soon enough, we can't stand it anymore and we go on the attack. When that backfires, we lapse into avoiding or accommodating.

None of these three common reactions serves our true interests. Once the fight-or-flight reaction gets triggered, the blood flows from our brain to our limbs, and our ability to think clearly diminishes. We forget our purpose and often act exactly contrary to our interests. When we react, we give away our power—our power to influence the other person constructively and to change the situation for the better. When we react, we are, in effect, saying *no* to our interests, *no* to ourselves.

But we have a choice. We don't need to react. We can learn to observe ourselves instead. In my teaching and writing, I emphasize the concept of *going to the balcony*. The balcony is a metaphor for a mental and emotional place of perspective, calm, and self-control. If life is a stage and we are all actors on that stage, then the balcony is a place from which we can see the entire play unfolding with greater clarity. To observe our selves, it is valuable to go to the balcony at all times, and especially before, during, and after any problematic conversation or negotiation.

I recall one tense political mediation session when the president of a country was shouting angrily at me for almost thirty minutes, accusing me of not seeing the tricks of the political opposition. What helped me keep calm was to silently take note of my sensations, emotions, and thoughts: *Isn't it interesting? My jaw feels clenched. I notice some fear showing up. My cheeks feel flushed. Am I feeling embarrassed?* Being able to recognize what I was feeling helped me to neutralize the emotional effect that the president's shouting had on me. I could watch the scene from the balcony as if it were a play. Having recovered myself, I was then able to recover the conversation with the president.

This is the point: whenever you feel yourself triggered by a passing thought, emotion, or sensation, you have a simple choice: *to identify* or *get identified*. You can observe the thought and "identify" it. Or you can let yourself get caught up in the thought, in other words, "get identified" with it. Naming helps you identify so that you don't get identified. As you observe your passing thoughts, emotions, and sensations, naming them—*Oh, that is my old friend Fear; there goes the Inner Critic*—neutralizes their effect on you and helps you to maintain your state of balance and calm. My friend Donna even likes to give humorous names to her reactive emotions such as "Freddy Fear," "Judge Judy," and "Anger Annie." (Humor, incidentally, can be a great ally in helping you regain perspective from the balcony.) As soon as you name the character in the play, you distance yourself from him or her.

Observing ourselves so that we don't react may seem easy,

but it is often tough to do, particularly in the heat of a difficult conversation or negotiation. As one business executive recently said to me, "I think of myself as a calm, cool person. And I am that way at work. But then sometimes, I find myself snapping at my wife. Why can't I stay calm like I am at work?" Like this husband, when our emotions get triggered, we all too often "fall off the balcony." If we want to be able to consistently rely on self-observation to keep us from reacting, it helps greatly to exercise it like a muscle on a daily basis.

Recently, I came across a mother's account of witnessing her own growing frustration in dealing with her four-year-old. Charlotte, the mother, wants to have a close and trusting relationship with her son, but his refusal to go to bed night after night triggers powerful reactions in her. Her account illustrates how difficult it is to resist the temptation to react and how practicing self-observation can help us make better choices. Charlotte writes:

Being both fascinated by and fearful of my new-found emotionality, I began to watch more closely what anger really felt like. The first thing I noticed was its seduction, its sexiness. There were times I could almost see myself at the emotional crossroads where one path led to calm, open-hearted resolution, the other to explosive anger. And it was hard, very hard at times, not to plunge down the latter. At the moment, giving expression to my anger felt like the thing I most wanted to do; its allure was profoundly powerful and overwhelmingly convincing.

Charlotte investigates with curiosity the strong temptation to explode at her child and gets a glimpse of the "crossroads," the point at which she can either give in to the anger or approach the situation in a calm way. If she gives in to her anger, her son will distance himself out of self-protection. If she remains calm, she can advance her core interest in a close and trusting relationship with him. What helps her maintain her state of balance is her ability to recognize the reactive pattern night after night, and to see that she actually has a choice *not* to react. As Charlotte realizes, self-observation is the foundation of self-mastery.

Try this yourself if you like. Investigate the feelings and reactive patterns that are triggered in you by a problematic relationship at home or at work. Notice the anger, fear, and other disturbing emotions that arise in you as you interact with the other person. Like Charlotte, learn to go to the balcony and observe these emotions and how they make you feel. See if you can spot your own crossroads, the moment in which you can choose between an impulsive reaction and a considered response that advances your true interests.

To develop a habit of self-observation, it helps to cultivate your *inner scientist*. You are the investigator, and the
subject of your investigation is yourself. Psychologists even
have a name for this: they call it "me-search." Approaching your thoughts and feelings with a spirit of inquiry—as
Charlotte does when she examines the feelings triggered
by her son's behavior—will help you keep your balance and
calm. Mastering the skill of observation requires, moreover,
that, like a good scientist, you observe the phenomenon
with detachment and an open mind. It requires that you
suspend self-judgment to the extent possible.

It is all too easy to judge our thoughts and emotions, to
see them as wrong or right, bad or good. But in a psychological sense, there is nothing really wrong that we can feel
or think. Actions can be wrong, but not thoughts or feelings. As inner scientists, we simply treat even the darker
thoughts and emotions as interesting research material. I
find a simple but powerful question to keep asking myself
is: "Isn't that *curious*?" The question creates distance and
opens the way to inquiry rather than judgment. As I have
cultivated my own practice of self-observation over the
years, I have come increasingly to appreciate the dictum
of the Indian philosopher Jiddu Krishnamurti: "To observe
without evaluating is the highest form of intelligence."

One way to train yourself to observe without judgment

is to reserve a period of time once a day—it could be as little as five or ten minutes—to sit quietly in a comfortable position, close your eyes, and simply watch your passing thoughts and feelings, almost as if the sky were observing the passing clouds. If you get caught up in a thought or feeling, or even if a harsh self-judgment shows up, treat it as perfectly fine. Simply notice that you were caught up and go back to observing. The more you engage in this exercise of mindfulness, the easier it becomes. Bit by bit, you familiarize yourself with the workings of your mind.

Imagine a glass of water that you have just filled from the faucet. It is full of fizz and you cannot see through it. If you wait a moment and let the water settle, however, the bubbles slowly dissipate and the water turns crystal clear. That is what we are trying to do here with our minds: to let the fizz settle so we can see clearly what is happening inside ourselves. Before a challenging phone call or meeting, I find benefit in taking even a single minute of silence to myself. One minute alone with my eyes closed helps me to observe my thoughts, feelings, and sensations and to quiet my mind so I can focus better in the conversation. It is an easy technique available to us at any time.

Learning to observe yourself is simple, but not easy, particularly in conflicts. With practice, you get better and better. Ideally, the balcony is not just a place to visit from time to time, but rather a home base. In your interactions with others, you can learn to be on the stage enacting the drama while at the same time watching it from the balcony. That takes practice, of course, but the more you can live your life with clarity and calm, the more effectively you will be able to deal with others and to pursue your interests with ease and success. The inner yes method is designed to help you go to the balcony when you like, stay on the balcony for as long as you like, and negotiate from a balcony perspective.

LISTEN WITH EMPATHY

Psychologists have estimated that we have anywhere between twelve thousand and sixty thousand thoughts a day. The majority of those—as high as 80 percent—are thought to be negative: obsessing about mistakes, battling guilt, or thinking about inadequacies. For some, the harsh critical voice of our inner judge is stronger, for others weaker, but perhaps no one escapes it. "You said the wrong thing!" "How could you have been so blind?" "You did a terrible job!" Each negative thought is a *no* to yourself. There is a saying that goes, "If you talked to your friends the way you talk to yourself, you wouldn't have any."

Self-judgment may be the greatest barrier to self-understanding. If we want to understand other human beings, there is no better way than to listen to them with empathy like a close friend would. If you wish to understand yourself, the same rule applies: listen with empathy. Instead of talking negatively to yourself, try to listen to yourself with respect and positive attention. Instead of judging yourself, accept yourself just as you are.

Empathy is often confused with sympathy, but it is different. Sympathy means "to feel *with*." It means to feel sorry for a person's predicament, but without necessarily understanding it. Empathy, in contrast, means "to feel *into*." It means to *understand* what it is like to be in that situation.

Listening to yourself with empathy goes one level deeper than observing. To observe is to *see from the outside,* whereas to listen is to *feel from the inside.* Observing offers you a detached view, whereas listening gives you an intimate understanding. Observation gives us the understanding of a scientist studying what a beetle looks like under a microscope, whereas listening gives you the understanding of what it feels like to be a beetle. You can benefit from both modalities together. Anthropologists have found that the best way to understand a foreign culture is to participate in it actively *and* at the same time to maintain an outside observer's perspective. I find this method, called participant observation, is equally useful when it comes to understanding ourselves.

As I listen to myself, I notice that the majority of my

problematic emotions are the same every day. For e:
one anxiety that pops up regularly concerns the daily to-
do list that only seems to expand: *Will I be able to get
through it?* To understand and reduce the intensity of these
recurring feelings, I have come up with a daily exercise:
In the morning, I imagine sitting at a kitchen table. As
each familiar thought or emotion such as anxiety or fear,
shame or pride shows up, I offer it an imaginary seat. I
have learned to welcome all customers, no one excluded.
I seek to treat them as the old friends or acquaintances
that they are. As the kitchen table fills up, I listen to the
free-flowing conversation of feelings and thoughts.

What about the inner judge? I make a place for him at
the kitchen table too. If I try to suppress or exclude him,
he simply goes underground and continues to judge from a
hiding place. The best approach, I find, is to simply accept
him as one of the regular characters in my life. I have even
come to appreciate him as being like an old uncle who
thinks he is trying to protect me but is often just getting in
the way. Accepting him, I find, is the best way to tame him.

If nothing else, I find this kitchen table exercise helps me
remain aware of these regulars so that they are less likely to
catch me by surprise and sweep me away. I have learned,
especially, to listen for any dark feelings or thoughts that I
may normally disown or stigmatize. Anger is one of them. I
have found that, if I don't recognize when I'm feeling angry

and then listen for what is behind that feeling, it can leak out in a destructive way when I least expect it, for example, in a sensitive conversation with my wife.

Jamil Mahuad, former president of Ecuador and a Harvard colleague, once shared how he gradually learned to deal with his painful feelings by putting these feelings in the spotlight. "Sadness . . . was not well received by males in my family. When some of my ancestors were really sad, they averted that emotion by expressing anger," he explained. "I had the same difficulty. Still it is not easy for me to connect with pain, with grief. But by recognizing and bringing this shadow to light, you start incorporating that 'new' part into what you are." By bringing his painful emotions "to light," Jamil was able to control his anger and operate with a balcony perspective as he conducted a difficult peace negotiation with the president of Peru, thereby putting an end to the longest-running war in the hemisphere.

Keep in mind that listening is not just an intellectual exercise but an emotional and physical one as well. For example, when you are afraid, try to feel the fear in your body. What does it feel like? Icy? Does it feel like a pit in your stomach? Does your throat feel parched? Recognize its familiar feeling and just stay with it for a moment without pushing it away. Try to relax and feel your way into the fear. Breathe into it if you can. That way, you can slowly begin to release it.

If this kind of deeper listening to yourself seems awkward or too challenging, consider asking a friend—or even a professional counselor or therapist—to listen to you until you are able to make a habit of listening to yourself. Or consider keeping a daily journal. I find that writing down my feelings and thoughts, even if only for a few minutes, keeps me on the balcony and helps me uncover patterns that I would not see in the rush of life. Try it out and you will begin to see and listen to yourself more clearly and understand yourself better.

One of the great benefits of listening to yourself before you enter into a problematic conversation or negotiation is that it clears your mind so that you can then listen far more easily to others. I have long taught listening as one of the central skills of negotiation and have noticed how difficult it is for people to listen to others, particularly in conflict situations. Could it be that the main obstacle is all the unheard emotions and thoughts that are clamoring for attention and cluttering up our minds? Could it be that the secret to listening to others is to listen to ourselves first?

UNCOVER YOUR NEEDS

If you listen to your feelings, particularly recurrent ones of dissatisfaction, you will find that they point you in the direction of unmet concerns and interests. Properly interpreted, they can help you uncover your deepest needs.

In the old story of King Arthur, a young knight from the court sets out with enthusiasm to find the Holy Grail. Within the first months of searching, he sees in the woods an apparition of a great castle. Entering, he finds an old injured king seated with his knights and on the banquet table a silver chalice, the very Grail itself. The young knight is tongue-tied, however, and while he wrestles with what to say to the king, the castle suddenly disappears and he is left alone in the forest, disconsolate.

The knight continues to search for many decades without success until one day there springs up in front of him the very same castle in the woods. The knight enters and sees the king and on the table the Grail. This time, much older and wiser, the knight instinctively finds the right words. He asks the old king a simple but powerful question: "What ails thee?" As the knight listens to the king's woes and uncovers his deepest needs, a human connection of friendship grows between the two and, out of that friendship, the king gives the knight the Grail, sought after by so many.

That is the power of asking the right question. We can each take a lesson from the knight and ask ourselves about what is not going well for us. In what areas of your life are you not happy or fully satisfied? Is it work or money, family or relationship, or health or general well-being? Feelings of dissatisfaction are the language that your needs use to communicate with you. When your needs are frustrated or unfulfilled, it is only natural to feel anxiety, fear, anger, or sadness. What, then, are these underlying needs? What do you most want? What are your deepest motivations? The better you understand your needs, the more likely you will be able to satisfy them.

I was once involved as a third party in a bitter civil war that had been going on in the jungles of Sumatra for twenty-five years. In a meeting with the leaders of the rebel movement, I asked them what they *really* wanted. "I know your *position* in this conflict. You want independence," I clarified. "But tell me more about what your *interests* are. *Why* do you want independence?" I still remember the uncomfortable silence that ensued as they struggled to answer this fundamental question.

Were they fighting chiefly for political reasons such as self-rule? Or economic reasons such as control over their natural resources? Or security reasons such as being able to defend themselves against a physical threat? Or cultural reasons such as the right to education in their own language? If they were fighting for more than one reason, what was their order of priority? The truth, as it emerged, was that, while they were crystal clear about their position—

independence—they were not as clear about the deeper motivations behind their fight for independence. Thousands had died in the struggle, but their leaders had not systematically articulated the underlying "why."

In my negotiation experience, I find that people usually know their *position:* "I want a 15 percent raise in salary." Often, however, they haven't thought deeply about their *interests*—their underlying needs, desires, concerns, fears, and aspirations: Do they want a raise because they are interested in recognition, or in fairness, or in career development, or in the satisfaction of some material need, or in a combination of these?

In negotiation, the magic question to uncover your true interests and needs is: "Why?" "*Why* do I want this?" One valuable practice is to keep asking yourself *why*—as many times as necessary—until you get down to your bedrock need. The deeper you go in uncovering your underlying needs and interests, the more likely you are to invent creative options that can satisfy your interests. In the case of the raise, for example, if your interest is in recognition, then even if budgetary constraints prevent your boss from giving you as high a raise as you had hoped, you might still be able to meet your interest by obtaining a new title or a prestigious assignment. Uncovering interests opens up new possibilities that you might not have thought of before.

In the case of the civil war, my colleagues and I delved deeply behind the rebels' position of independence and into their underlying interests. Using a flipchart, I started writing down their answers to the *why* question: self-rule, control over their economic resources, preservation of their culture and language, and so on. The next question I asked was: "What strategy will best serve these interests?" Would it be to continue to wage war? The rebel commanders readily acknowledged that, because the government army was strong, the war could not be won even in ten years. Or would the best strategy be to form a political party and run for office?

It took some years for the rebel movement to debate and eventually choose the second political route. When they did, they negotiated a peace agreement with the government that gave them self-rule, control over their resources, and cultural rights. When the provincial elections were held, rebel commanders became the governor and vice-governor. While they did not obtain independence, they nonetheless advanced their strategic interests. That is the power of uncovering and focusing on your true interests.

The deeper we go in probing for our own underlying needs, the more universal those needs tend to become:

"Why do you want the raise?"

"To have more money."

"Why do you want more money?"

"So I can get married."

"Why do you want to get married?"

"Because it will bring me love."

"Why do you want to be loved?"

"To be happy, of course."

The bedrock desire then, is a universal one: to be loved and happy. This may seem utterly obvious, but uncovering this universal desire can actually open up a new line of internal inquiry. If you don't get the raise at the level you want, can you still be happy? Does your happiness depend on the raise—or even on the marriage—or does it come from you, from inside? It is not an idle question. To the extent that you can find a way to experience love and happiness from the inside, you will be more likely to find love and happiness if you get married *or* if you don't, if you get the raise *or* if you don't.

Among our basic psychological needs, two universal ones stand out in particular. One is *protection,* or safety, which promises the absence of pain. Another is *connection,* or love, which promises the presence of pleasure. How can we protect and connect? Since life is, by nature, insecure and since love often feels insufficient, it is not always easy for us to meet these needs fully. But we can begin the process.

FROM SELF-JUDGMENT TO SELF-UNDERSTANDING

As straightforward and natural as it sounds, it is often not that easy to put yourself in your own shoes—to see yourself from the balcony, to listen to yourself with empathy, and to uncover your underlying needs. The journey from self-judgment to self-understanding takes hard and continual work.

To return to the earlier example I gave of my client Abilio Diniz, even once he had uncovered his deepest need—freedom—he encountered many internal difficulties in his way. Shortly after our conversation, Abilio gave a major and lengthy magazine interview in which he emphasized that he was moving beyond the battle with his former business partner in order to live his life. In the introduction to the article, however, the interviewer noted that, in the course of the conversation, Abilio mentioned his adversary by his full name thirty-eight times, hardly an indication of moving ahead. The following week, Abilio was in a board meeting of his organization and, despite his expressed intention to keep his cool, felt provoked and repeatedly called his opponents cowards. However much he tried, he found it hard to stay on the balcony.

When I next spoke with Abilio, who was becoming a friend in the process of our work together, he told me:

"The truth is that I am still furious. What can I do? I don't know what I really want. Sometimes it is to finish the dispute and sometimes it is to carry on the fight. I may have no choice anyway but to continue to fight. Maybe I should just enjoy it."

The process of getting to yes with yourself can often be difficult just as it was for Abilio. In the problematic situations we face at work, at home, or in the larger world, it is common to be torn and undecided and it is easy to continue to react. That is why the patient and courageous practice of putting yourself in your shoes is so vital. Abilio persisted. He had long intimate talks about his dilemma with his wife and family. He went every week to see a therapist to uncover his darkest feelings. He talked with me. He wrestled with his temper; and with dedication and discipline, he learned to spend more time on the balcony. By understanding and accepting himself just as he was, he became his own ally rather than his own worst opponent.

However challenging it was for Abilio to engage in this psychological work of figuring out what he really wanted and then reaching an inner agreement with himself, in the end the rewards were immensely greater: he received his life back. Even before we approached his opponent at the negotiation table, Abilio took concrete actions to pursue his freedom. He became chair of the board of another major company, he found a new office outside of the company headquarters, he went on a prolonged holiday with his family, and he began to explore a new business deal. In other words, he said *yes* to his needs. This *yes* to himself opened up the possibility of approaching his adversary for a genuine negotiation, one in which neither side would lose. And that made all the difference, as we'll see later in the book.

As this story suggests, putting yourself in your shoes helps you become your friend rather than your opponent when it comes to negotiating with others. It helps you not only to understand yourself, but to accept yourself just as you are. If self-judgment is a *no* to self, self-acceptance is a *yes* to self, perhaps the greatest gift we can give ourselves. Some might worry that accepting themselves as they are will diminish the motivation to make positive changes, but I have found that the exact opposite is usually true. Acceptance can create the sense of safety within which we can more easily face a problem and work on it. As Carl Rogers, one of the founders of humanistic psychology, once noted: "The curious paradox is that when I accept myself as I am, then I change."

Now that you have put yourself in your shoes and uncovered your needs, the natural question to ask is: Where can you find the power to meet those needs? That is the next challenge in getting to yes with yourself.

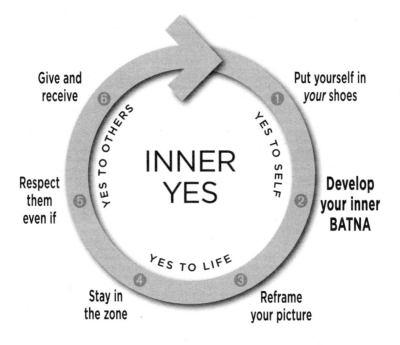

Give and receive ⑥

Put yourself in *your* shoes ①

YES TO OTHERS

YES TO SELF

INNER YES

Respect them even if ⑤

Develop your inner BATNA ②

YES TO LIFE

Stay in the zone ④

Reframe your picture ③

DEVELOP YOUR INNER BATNA

FROM BLAME TO SELF-RESPONSIBILITY

I saw too many people give away their last morsel
of food, their last sip of water to others in need
to know that no one can take away the last of
our human freedoms—the freedom to choose our
own way, in whatever the circumstances.

—DR. VIKTOR FRANKL, *MAN'S SEARCH FOR MEANING,*
ON HIS EXPERIENCES IN NAZI CONCENTRATION CAMPS

In the mid-1980s, I helped facilitate a series of confer-
ences between top Soviet and American policy advisers
on the question of how to prevent a nuclear war. The
times were tense and the accusations were flying back
and forth between the two superpowers. Each time we
held a meeting, the first session began with a long laun-

dry list of attacks and defensive arguments. It poisoned the atmosphere and took up a lot of valuable time. By the third or fourth such conference, my colleagues and I tried a different tack. On the printed agenda, we labeled the subject of the first meeting "Mutual Accusations" and scheduled it before breakfast for anyone who wanted to show up. Everyone got the point.

The blame game is the core pattern of almost every destructive conflict I have ever witnessed. The husband blames the wife and vice versa. Management blames the union and vice versa. One political enemy blames the other and vice versa. Blaming usually triggers feelings of anger or shame in the other, which provokes counterblame. And on it goes.

It is so tempting to blame those with whom we are in conflict. Who started the argument, after all, if it wasn't the other person? Blaming makes us feel innocent. We are the ones who were wronged. We get to feel righteous and even superior. And blaming also nicely deflects any residual guilt we might feel. The emotional benefits are clear.

But, as I have witnessed in countless conflicts over the years, the costs of the blame game are huge. It escalates disputes needlessly and prevents us from resolving them. It poisons relationships and wastes valuable time and energy. Perhaps most insidiously, it undermines our power: when we blame others for what is wrong in the relationship—whether it is a marital dispute, an office spat, or a superpower clash—we are dwelling on their power and our victimhood. We are overlooking whatever part we may have played in the conflict and are ignoring our freedom to choose how to respond. We are giving our power away.

If we want to get to yes with others, particularly in the more difficult situations we face every day, we need to find a way to get past the blame game. We need to reclaim our power to change the situation for the better. While I was working on the problem of preventing nuclear crises between the United States and the Soviet Union, I studied crisis management in other areas of life such as business. At the time, the most striking example of a successful response to a dire situation was the way the pharmaceutical company Johnson and Johnson responded to the Tylenol crisis in 1982. Today, Johnson and Johnson's response has become a classic case study, but back when it took place, the company's approach was truly eye-opening. The top news story in the nation day after day, week after week, was the deaths by poisoning of six adults and one child who had ingested Tylenol laced with cyanide in the Chicago area. No one knew who had taken the capsules and injected them with poison. CEO James Burke was faced with the dilemma of how to respond. Tylenol was the company's most profitable product, commanding 37 percent of the market in over-the-counter painkillers.

Many experts cautioned against a nationwide recall, arguing that the incidents were limited to the Chicago area and that the poisoning was not the fault of Johnson and Johnson. But Burke and his colleagues chose not to take the easy way out by placing the responsibility for their customers' safety elsewhere. Instead, they assumed full responsibility, ordered the product withdrawn from the shelves of drugstores across the country, and offered to exchange all the existing Tylenol capsules in people's homes for Tylenol tablets. This one decision, made almost immediately after the deaths were reported, cost the company an estimated hundred million dollars.

The result? Contrary to conventional wisdom at the time, which held that there was no way the Tylenol brand could possibly recover from such a widely publicized disaster, Tylenol was relaunched within months under the same name in a new tamper-resistant bottle and went on to achieve an astonishing recovery in sales and market share. What could easily have turned into a devastating crisis in public confidence became a confirmation in the public's eyes of Johnson and Johnson's integrity and credibility.

The opposite of the blame game is to take responsibility. By responsibility, I mean "response-ability"—the ability to respond constructively to a situation facing us, treating it as ours to handle. That is what James Burke and his colleagues at Johnson and Johnson did. No matter how challenging or costly it might be, taking responsibility, they knew, lies at the heart of genuine leadership. And the rewards were great: taking responsibility made it possible to get to a *yes* in the form of restored confidence with doctors, nurses, patients, and other stakeholders.

Once you get past the blame game and take responsibility, it becomes much easier for you to get to *yes* with others. The real work starts from within. Taking responsibility means taking responsibility for your *life* and your *relationships*. And, perhaps most important, it means making an unconditional commitment to take care of your *needs*.

OWN YOUR LIFE

It seems like a simple question—Who is really responsible for our lives?—but somehow the answer eludes us more frequently than we would like. Even though intellectually we know that *we* are responsible for our words, our actions, and even our reactions, we often look at our lives, wondering how we got where we are and typically find the answer in external factors: "I'm not where I want to be in my career because my boss hates me and has blocked my advancement." "I can't travel because I don't have the money." "I live here instead of the city where I really want to live because my family pressured me to stay." In other words, it was not our decision; someone else or some external circumstance is to blame.

I recall the story of Sam, a young friend of mine who kept getting into car accidents. First, he destroyed the family van beyond repair . . . then the family jeep . . . then his own car. Thankfully, he was not injured nor was anyone else. Each time, he would get angry and blame the accident on circumstances beyond his control—the other driver, the conditions on the road, a poorly lit sign. *He* was not responsible, that was very clear to him. The string of accidents combined with his lack of responsibility alarmed Sam's parents and led to tension and conflict in the family.

Finally, after a process of observing himself closely and listening to his underlying feelings, Sam came to the realization that the repetitive pattern of accidents might be related to his aggressive driving. Probing more deeply, he came to understand how this aggressive tendency arose from suppressed feelings of insecurity and anger. He came to accept those feelings, which led him to take full responsibility for his driving as well as for the accidents, even those that seemed like genuine ones. Perhaps most important, he finally understood that *he*—and he alone—was responsible for his life and what happened in it. Once he was able to get to yes with himself in this way, he was able to get to yes with his parents. And, perhaps not surprisingly, the pattern of automobile accidents utterly ceased.

That is the power of self-responsibility when twinned with self-understanding. Self-understanding without self-responsibility runs the risk of dissolving into self-pity. Self-responsibility without self-understanding can deteriorate into self-blame. To get to yes with yourself, you need both. As Sam's story makes clear, the work of putting yourself in your shoes gives you the understanding to then take responsibility for your life and your actions.

Taking responsibility for your life means owning your failures and faults as well as your successes and strengths. It takes honesty and courage to do so, but only then will you be able to say that you have put yourself genuinely in your own shoes. You can then occupy your shoes fully—holes and all. Whereas self-responsibility is often confused with self-blame, it is, in fact, quite the opposite. Self-blame looks backward, judging what is past: "What a failure I have been at work!" Self-responsibility looks essentially forward, figuring out how to address the problem. "What can I do to make my work successful?"

If our life is a play, we may not be the playwright, but

we can choose to be the director. We can interpret the play as we choose, able to portray ourselves either as victims of destiny or as the captains of our fate. Whether what happens to us is pure accident or not, we are the decisive factor in our life: we may not always be able to choose our circumstances, but we are able to choose our responses to them.

When my friend Jerry White was a college student studying abroad in Jerusalem, he went on a camping trip in the Golan Heights and stepped on a land mine left behind from the Six-Day War. He lost his leg—and almost his life. As he lay in bed in a hospital for months on end, with alternating feelings of grief, anger, bitterness, and self-pity, a soldier lying in a bed next to him said: "Jerry, this will be the worst thing that ever happened to you or the best thing. You decide."

Jerry took the soldier's advice and chose *not* to settle into the role of a victim blaming others and life itself for his difficulties. Instead Jerry chose to take responsibility for his life and to change his circumstances. "I didn't like that image of myself—bitter, whiny Jerry who let a bad thing take over the rest of his life," Jerry wrote in his inspiring book *I Will Not Be Broken*. "There is a life to be lived—my life—and if I had to hop, roll, or whatever, I was going to get back to it." In effect, Jerry said *yes* to himself and his life.

It was not always easy for him, of course, but Jerry responded to his accident by giving his life to service. Eventually he cofounded Survivor Corps, a global network of land-mine survivors who help victims of war and terror, which played a leading role in the Nobel Prize–winning International Campaign to Ban Landmines. From there, Jerry went into public service, working on resolving conflicts around the world. Getting to yes with himself helped him get to yes with others—and indeed his lifework turned to helping entire societies get to yes.

Jerry shifted how he saw himself in the play—from the role of powerless victim to the role of leader. Like Jerry, each of us has the ability to reframe the guiding question from "Who is to blame?" to "What do we have to learn?" When faced with adversity, we can either blame others or life for our current circumstances or we can become curious and ask ourselves what lesson life is bringing us. Instead of resisting our current circumstances we can take responsibility for our lives as they are right now. Even if we would prefer not to face a particular challenge, we can choose the challenge anyway simply because it is what is in front of us. Instead of lamenting our fate, we can, like Jerry, choose to embrace it.

Even if, objectively speaking, we are only partly in control of our circumstances, we still have considerable control over our *experiences*. Like Jerry, we can choose how we interpret what happens to us, no matter how bad, which will directly influence how we continue to feel about it and how we respond. If a business deal turns sour, we can choose to blame others and stew in our resentment and anger, or we can choose to see it as an occasion to learn and move on to a new deal. If a spouse or partner leaves, we can blame him or her and let that decision define our experience, or we can listen to our feelings, accept them, take ownership of our lives, and move forward.

Perhaps no one has expressed the truth of our power to choose more vividly than Dr. Viktor Frankl in *Man's Search for Meaning,* his wrenching and poignant account of his own experiences as an inmate for three years in Auschwitz, Dachau, and other Nazi concentration camps. As he learned in the hardest way, even when we are utterly deprived of freedom, we remain free in the end to give our experience the meaning that we choose. In the midst of unimaginable suffering, he chose to take responsibility for his life and his experience. He reached out and helped people in need, giving them solace and whatever little nourishment he could spare. In a situation where seemingly he had no power, he reclaimed the power to govern his own life.

Taking responsibility for our lives may seem heavy at times, but in fact it can be liberating. It can free up enormous energies that have long been trapped in the drama of blaming others as well as ourselves. It is the blame game, the absence of responsibility, which keeps us imprisoned as victims. The moment we recognize that we are in a prison of our own making, the walls begin to crumble and we are free. By owning our lives, we can start living them to the full.

OWN YOUR RELATIONSHIPS

If the blame game lies at the root of most of the conflicts I have ever witnessed, taking responsibility for the relationship lies at the root of most of the truly successful resolutions I have ever seen.

Think of your relationship with someone at home, at work, or in the community that has been problematic for you. Have you ever felt tempted to blame the other person and to cast yourself in the role of victim? It is all too common to blame others for negative aspects of a relationship with them. But, as we all know, every relationship—and every conflict—has at least two parties.

In his insightful book *Passionate Marriage,* psychologist Dr. David Schnarch presents the case of a client named Susan, a woman with a strong need for communicating and connecting with others, who was unhappily married to Frank. As she saw it, she and Frank rarely, if ever, really talked. For years, Susan had criticized and nagged Frank into talking with her but, the more she did, the more he retreated into his shell. She felt it was his fault that they couldn't move forward on this challenge in their relationship. She was angry and frustrated because she could not get to the yes she wanted with her husband.

With the help of her therapist, Susan was able to put herself in her own shoes and learned to understand and accept herself as she was—someone who wanted to connect deeply with others by talking and sharing feelings. Then she learned to understand her husband—someone who did not like talking and sharing feelings. She finally realized how she contributed to their negative dynamic, recognizing that her nagging only accentuated Frank's withdrawal. Frank had suffered a lot of trauma in his childhood, so he did not feel safe opening up. In fact, the more Susan criticized him, the less safe he felt and the more he would clam up.

In the end, others' shortcomings must be considered *their* problem, not yours. Your challenge is how to respond. You can choose to acknowledge your contribution to the problematic relationship, as Susan did. Even if your contribution seems relatively small in your eyes, especially when compared to the other person's, it is still a contribution. And if you look truly honestly at the situation, as Susan was able to do, you may see that your contribution is not so small after all. There is an old saying that when you point your finger at someone, three fingers point back at you. It is not about blaming yourself, but simply realizing that you have a part in the relationship and the problem. Rather than get lost in the blame game, it is more useful to realize that it takes two to create the mess—and only one to begin to transform the relationship. By taking responsibility for your relationship, you reclaim your power to change it.

Taking responsibility for the state of your relationship also means recognizing when your words or actions have caused harm or distress. In my work as a mediator in conflicts ranging from business battles to ethnic wars, I have seen the power of a sincere apology to help heal a rift in the relationship. I recall one occasion when I was facilitating a confidential meeting in Europe between Turkish and Kurdish opinion leaders at a time when a civil war was raging in Turkey. A retired Turkish general asked to speak: "As a former leader of the armed forces of Turkey, I want to acknowledge the suffering of countless Kurdish villagers during the course of this terrible war. I know that many innocents have died and been injured. And, personally, I want to say that I am profoundly sorry." The tension in the meetings had been great but this one sincere statement dramatically changed the atmosphere and opened the way for an eventual agreement to work together to end the war. What makes an apology successful is the invisible work beforehand, in this case, the general coming to own his actions and the role he played in the conflict before offering the apology. The success of the apology depends critically on the work inside.

OWN YOUR NEEDS

In *Getting to Yes,* Roger Fisher and I argued that your greatest source of power in a negotiation is your BATNA—your Best Alternative To a Negotiated Agreement. Your BATNA is your best course of action for satisfying your interests if you cannot reach agreement with the other side. If you are negotiating a new job offer, for example, your best alternative might be to seek another job offer. In the case of a contractual dispute, your best alternative to negotiation might be to resort to a mediator or take the matter to court. If you cannot agree on a price with one car dealer, you can find another dealer. Your BATNA gives you the confidence that, no matter what happens in the negotiation, you have a good alternative. It makes you less dependent on the other side to satisfy your needs. It gives you a sense of freedom as well as power and confidence.

For thirty-five years, I have been teaching people to identify and develop their BATNAs. Yet, as I have seen, it is often challenging for people as they discover that their alternatives are not at all obvious or are quite unattractive: "I can't find another job." "Going to court will cost a lot of time and money." Faced with a negotiating counterpart who appears more powerful, many people struggle to equalize the power balance.

We can, however, increase our power from within in a way that is always available to us, no matter what our outer situations might be. In a negotiation or conflict, well before we develop an *external* alternative to a negotiated agreement, we can create an *internal* alternative to a negotiated agreement. We can make a strong unconditional commitment to ourselves to take care of our deepest needs, *no matter what* other people do or don't do. That commitment is our inner BATNA. Genuine power starts inside of us.

In the example of a job offer negotiation, while your outer BATNA might be to seek and accept another job offer, your inner BATNA is your commitment to yourself that, regardless of whether you successfully negotiate this job offer (or another job offer, for that matter), *you* will take care of your needs for satisfaction and fulfillment in your work no matter what.

The key phrase is *no matter what*. Your inner BATNA is your commitment to stop blaming yourself, others, and life itself for your dissatisfactions *no matter what*. It is your commitment to remove the responsibility for meeting your true needs from the other person's shoulders—and to assume it yourself *no matter what*. This unconditional commitment gives you the motivation and the power to change your circumstances, especially in a difficult situation or conflict. Your inner BATNA is, in effect, the foundation for your outer BATNA.

In Susan's case, which I described in the previous section, she realized that she was choosing to stay in this deeply unsatisfying relationship *and* that she could choose to leave. Leaving was a last resort, of course, something she very much preferred not to do. Leaving was, in negotiation terms, her outer BATNA, her best course of action for satisfying her needs *if* she could not reach agreement with her husband, Frank. Having taken responsibility for her role in the dynamics of the relationship, Susan took responsibility for her needs. She developed her inner BATNA, making an unconditional commitment to herself to take care of her needs no matter what. She was thus able to approach her husband in an entirely new way. She calmly informed Frank:

I'm no longer willing to accept how rarely we talk, and I'm no longer willing to push you to do it. But don't assume I'm accepting things the way they are because I won't be nagging or criticizing you anymore. For myself, I don't want to be pathetically grateful just because my partner talks to me. . . . And for you, I don't want you feeling pressured all the time by a screeching wife. I'll interpret what you do from here on as indicating your decision about how you really want to live. I'll make my decision about my life accordingly.

Susan gave up trying to control her husband's behavior, which was having the opposite effect she intended. Instead, she took responsibility for her needs and chose how *she* would act. She committed herself to living a more connected and satisfying way of life, regardless of how Frank continued to behave. She showed respect to Frank, allowing him to make his own decisions, and at the same time, she showed respect to herself, reclaiming her autonomy.

Although on the surface, Susan's approach might appear to have threatened her marriage, it actually had the opposite effect. Assuming responsibility for her actions and her future enabled Susan to stop her destructive habit of criticizing Frank. And when the criticism stopped, Frank felt safe and was willing to open up and talk more about his feelings and needs. Their marriage was not only saved, but transformed. Susan got to yes—with herself and with Frank.

The more we need another person to satisfy our needs, the more power that individual has over us, the more dependent and needy we are likely to behave. Taking responsibility for our needs not only helps us, but can also, as Susan's story illustrates, facilitate the process of getting to yes with the other person. Whereas our outer BATNA is subject to change, our inner BATNA, that commitment to take care of ourselves, is always there and can never be taken from us. In my years of teaching about negotiation, what I have come to realize is that the best BATNA of all, the one that can give us the most confidence and power in a conflict situation, is the one that starts inside. It is a missing key to success in negotiation.

In life, we are destined to deal with many difficult situations. A domineering boss insists we work nights and weekends; we acquiesce, telling ourselves we need the job. An ornery client constantly demands last-minute changes and concessions; we give in, telling ourselves we need that business. A teenage daughter refuses to listen to our admonitions and disrespects us; we ignore her behavior, telling ourselves we need her love. In these difficult situations, we may see no alternative but to accept ill treatment from others. It is all too easy to fall into the trap of making ourselves emotional prisoners of others.

In the end, each of us must answer the question "*Who is responsible for meeting my core psychological needs?*" If we answer, "someone else," we will give our power away to them. But, if we answer, "ourselves," we can reclaim the power to change our life and our future.

FROM BLAME TO SELF-RESPONSIBILITY

I learned the lesson of self-responsibility in perhaps the most personally challenging situation and set of negotiations I have ever had to face, which was with the doctors and nurses on whom the life and health of my daughter, Gabriela, depended. Gabi, as we call her, was born with a series of congenital anomalies called VATER syndrome that affected her spine, her spinal cord, her feet, and some of her organs. She required urgent medical attention from the day she was born and over the years went through fourteen major surgeries. It was not clear in the beginning whether she would ever walk or even live. What was hardest, naturally, for my wife, Lizanne, and me was to watch her suffer. We feared for her life, her health, and her well-being.

We were tempted to find something to blame for Gabi's suffering and the ordeal we were going through—ourselves, unresponsive or insensitive doctors, or even life itself. But, as we learned, there was no use in blaming anyone or anything. The only healthy way forward was to take responsibility for our life just as it was, for our relationships with doctors and nurses, and for our own psychological needs.

With the help of a friend who was a therapist, we first learned to put ourselves in our shoes. Both Lizanne and I have a tendency to act strong and to skirt the places of inner pain. But, as we went first to the balcony and then listened to ourselves, we let ourselves feel our emotions of fear, dread, anxiety, guilt, shame, and anger, emotions that I at least had numbed. We learned to give ourselves and each other empathy and compassion, especially when facing a difficult and dangerous surgery. We found that by deliberately facing our pain, imagining our worst fears of losing Gabi, entering the fear rather than steering around it, we were able to go through it and ultimately experience emotional relief and healing. Although every protective instinct urged us to go around the pain, the key lesson we learned is that *the way forward is through.*

The work of self-understanding helped us to take responsibility for our circumstances. We learned to accept life the way it was, not to resist it or to lose time and energy wishing it were different. We took response-ability and sought to do the best we could to help Gabi, the family, and ourselves. We looked for every occasion to lead a normal, healthy family life with lots of laughter and love. We treated Gabi like her brothers and encouraged her to live life as fully as possible, going out for sports she liked, even if they were more challenging for her given her physical condition. Here Gabi was our best teacher since she never saw herself as a victim, never indulged in self-pity, but sought to make each day fun for herself. Although we would never have voluntarily chosen such an ordeal for Gabi and for us, we said *yes* to the situation rather than *no*. In this way, we took back our life, our initiative, and our power to change the situation for the better.

We also learned to take responsibility for our relationships with doctors and nurses. Even if medical specialists were insensitive, we learned not to blame them but to take the initiative to address the problem. Just before Gabi's spinal cord surgery, for example, one doctor casually announced to his students in front of Lizanne, who was cradling five-month-old Gabi in her arms: "I've seen many kids go into this surgery and come out paraplegic." We were shocked by his callousness. Not long thereafter, we were referred to this same doctor as the most skilled surgeon in town for another of Gabi's surgeries. Although we might easily have dismissed him because of our first encounter with him, we went to the balcony and focused on what was best for Gabi. In the end, we created a good relationship with him and he eventually became a friend, offering us hours and hours of free consultation about numerous surgeries, and taking close care of Gabi.

What helped us conduct these critical relationships was our commitment to ourselves to take care of our own psychological needs. Doing so allowed us to control our levels of anxiety around Gabi's surgeries. The less anxious we were, the more trusting, calm, and confident Gabi also became since she was very much relying on us to see whether she should be afraid or not and whether she should trust or not. The less anxious Gabi and we became, the easier we found it to deal nonreactively with doctors and nurses who were sometimes brusque and unresponsive.

It was a big lesson for us. We had thought we were wholly dependent on the medical system, but the more responsibility we took and the more confidence we developed in ourselves and in life, the more relaxed we could be and therefore the more effectively we could serve as Gabi's advocates. Everyone benefited. Getting to yes with ourselves helped us get to yes with the people on whom Gabi's life depended.

As Lizanne and I learned, taking responsibility for meeting your needs is fundamentally about *self-leadership*. All too often, the inner judge, the constant critic, tries to take charge, using fear and blame, guilt and shame as instruments of control. Taking responsibility allows you to carry out an inner revolution of sorts. You can displace the judge and assume your rightful place as leader of your own life.

The key lesson is that responsibility equals power, power to meet your deepest needs. In the end, each of us is faced with a basic choice of attitude. If blaming essentially means giving away your power and thus saying *no* to yourself, taking responsibility means reclaiming your power and thus saying *yes* to yourself. By giving up the blame game and assuming responsibility for your relationships and your needs, you can go right to the root of conflict and take the lead in transforming your negotiations and your life.

This brings us to the next challenge in getting to yes with ourselves. While we can choose to take responsibility for our needs, the question remains: Where can we find a source of satisfaction to meet our deepest needs for connection and protection? For that, we turn to the next major attitudinal shift: to say *yes* to the life that sustains us. Having said *yes* to ourselves, we are now ready to say *yes* to life.

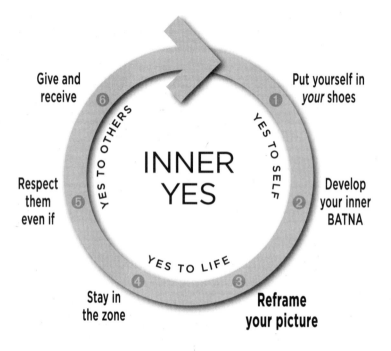

Give and receive
6

Put yourself in *your* shoes
1

YES TO OTHERS

YES TO SELF

INNER YES

Respect them even if
5

Develop your inner BATNA
2

YES TO LIFE

Stay in the zone
4

Reframe your picture
3

REFRAME YOUR PICTURE

FROM UNFRIENDLY TO FRIENDLY

Nothing can bring you peace but yourself.

—RALPH WALDO EMERSON

In the wake of World War II and the advent of the atomic bomb, Albert Einstein posed what he believed was the most important question for each of us: "Is the universe a friendly place?" "This," Einstein declared, "is the first and most basic question all people must answer for themselves."

Einstein reasoned that, if we see the universe as basically hostile, we will naturally treat others as enemies. On the collective level, we will arm ourselves to the teeth and react at the first provocation. Given the weapons of mass destruction at our disposal, we will eventually destroy ourselves as well as all life on Earth. If we see the universe as friendly, however, we are more likely to treat others as potential partners. We are thus more likely to get to yes with others, beginning with those closest to us at home, at work, and in the community—and then extending the process out to humanity itself. In other words, the answer we give to this all-important question is self-confirming. Depending on our response, we will behave differently and our interactions will likely have diametrically different outcomes.

In my negotiation classes, I teach about the power of reframing, the capacity each of us has to give a different interpretation or meaning to the situation. In every challenging conversation or negotiation, we have a choice: Do we approach the negotiation as an adversarial contest in which one party wins and the other loses? Or do we approach it instead as an opportunity for collaborative problem solving in which both sides can benefit? We have the ability to reframe each difficult conversation from an adversarial confrontation into a cooperative interchange between partners. The best way to change the game is to change the frame.

But reframing isn't always easy. Even when we see the merits of a win-win approach to negotiations, it is all too easy in the heat of a conflict to fall into the trap of win-lose thinking and to see the other side—a boss, a colleague, a client, even a spouse or child—as an adversary in a fight for scarce resources, whether it is money, attention, or power. Almost everyone has a fear of scarcity, and when that fear dominates us, getting to yes becomes tough.

So where can we get some help to be able to reframe? As I have come increasingly to appreciate, the ability to reframe the *external* situation comes first from an ability to reframe our *internal* picture of life. If we truly wish to shift from an adversarial to a cooperative approach in our interactions with others, we would do well to ask ourselves Einstein's fundamental question. What is our working assumption? Can we think, act, and conduct our relationships as if the universe is essentially a friendly place and life is, in fact, on our side?

It is not always easy, particularly in the midst of adversity, to see life as being on our side. During the time I was writing this book, I was serving as a negotiation adviser to the president of a country that was afflicted by a long-running guerrilla war in which hundreds of thousands had died and millions had become refugees. The president wanted to start peace talks in order to explore the possibility of a negotiated end to the war, but there was a great deal of political opposition to the idea of talking with the guerrillas who were branded as "terrorists." The president wanted an agreement on a clear and limited agenda with the guerrillas before he would announce the beginning of peace talks; and, in order to reach this preliminary agreement, secret in-depth conversations needed to take place with the guerrilla leadership.

The president and his team were faced with a problem: how could they "extract" a guerrilla commander from his jungle headquarters and fly him to a third country where these preliminary secret talks could be held without anyone's knowledge? No one could find out about this operation—not the media, not the police, and not even the army, who would certainly try to destroy the guerrilla headquarters if they knew where it was. For this highly delicate and dangerous mission, the president charged a man I will call James. James's task was to hire a private helicopter and fly in it to a secret meeting place in the middle of a jungle clearing to pick up the commander.

When James's helicopter finally landed in the designated location, no one was there, but, within minutes, it was swarmed by hundreds of guerrillas emerging from the jungle, each carrying an AK-47 machine gun, all of which were aimed directly at the helicopter with James inside it. He could hear many of the guerrillas shouting excitedly to their commander that this whole arrangement was a fatal trick. The level of tension and distrust was extremely high.

It is not hard to imagine just how hostile and frightening the situation must have seemed to James. What could he do to defuse the situation? Some days after the event, he told me that after a few moments of sitting in the helicopter, nervous and unsure of what to do next, he had an idea. He opened the door, stepped out of the helicopter, walked boldly up to the enemy commander, stretched out his hand, and confidently announced: "Sir, I am now placing you under the personal protection of the president!"

In that tense moment when James found himself the target of hundreds of machine guns, he had a choice: he could choose to see the other side as hostile—and given the circumstances few of us would fault him if he did—or he could choose to see the other side as his partner. James chose the latter, and because he treated the enemy commander as a partner, the commander was able to treat him as a partner too. After a brief pause to say good-bye to his comrades, the commander boarded the helicopter, and the secret preliminary peace talks began soon thereafter in a foreign capital. Six months later, a preliminary agreement in principle was announced and full-fledged peace negotiations began.

I asked James what gave him the ability to reframe that dangerous situation and he told me he had a fundamental trust in life, an assumption that it would all somehow work out. Because he saw life as his ally, James could see the commander as his unlikely partner.

If, like James, we can learn to reframe our picture of life as essentially friendly even in the face of adversity, we will not only be able to get to yes with ourselves but will have a much better chance of getting to yes with others. In reframing your picture of life, three practices can help, in my experience. First, remember your connection to life. Second, remember your power to make your own happiness. Third, learn to appreciate the lessons that life brings you.

REMEMBER YOUR CONNECTION TO LIFE

"A human being," Einstein once wrote, "is part of the whole called by us 'Universe,' a part limited in time and space. He experiences himself, his thoughts and feelings as something separated from the rest, a kind of optical delusion of his consciousness . . ."

My original training was in anthropology—the study of human nature and culture. As I learned in my studies, the interconnectedness of human beings is an anthropological truth. We are not separate at all, as Einstein points out, but rather inextricably woven into a larger web of human and other living beings. We are intimately connected to the whole biologically, economically, socially, and culturally. We know this truth scientifically, but it is often hard for us to appreciate it fully. We all too easily forget our connection to life.

Sometimes it takes a real shock for us to see through Einstein's optical delusion. Dr. Jill Bolte Taylor, a Harvard neuroanatomist, suffered a stroke at the age of thirty-seven that flooded and disabled the left hemisphere of her brain. "How many brain scientists have the opportunity to study their own brain from the inside out?" she shared at a celebrated TED talk. "In the course of four hours, I watched my brain completely deteriorate in its ability to process all information. On the morning of the hemorrhage, I could not walk, talk, read, write or recall any of my life."

At the same time, to her great surprise, Taylor began to feel a sense of euphoric happiness as she shed the stress and anxieties of her life. "Imagine what it would be like to be totally disconnected from your brain chatter," she told the TED audience. "I felt a sense of peacefulness." Her sense of separateness—the optical delusion—vanished and she felt connected to life. Without intending it, she had reframed her picture of life from unfriendly to friendly.

It took Taylor eight long years to recover from the stroke.

It was slow and difficult, but her desire to teach others about the state of happiness and peace that she had found kept her motivated. Taylor came to understand what had happened to her in terms of the strikingly different functions of the two halves of the brain.

Generally speaking, the left side of our brain is responsible for language, logic, judgment, and a sense of time, the tools we need to navigate our daily lives. "Our left brain thinks linearly, creates and understands language, defines the boundaries of where we begin and where we end, judges what is right and wrong and is a master of details, details and more details about those details . . . It focuses on our differences and specializes in critical judgment of those unlike ourselves . . ." Taylor writes. This is the side of Taylor's brain that was affected during her stroke.

If the left side of the brain is responsible for our sense that we are separate and different from others, the right side gives us a sense of connection to life and to others. "Our right mind focuses on our similarities, the present moment, inflection of voice, and the bigger picture of how we are all connected. Because it focuses on our similarities . . . [our right brain] is compassionate, expansive, open, and supportive of others," Taylor writes.

Clearly, we need our left brain to help us navigate in the world and to protect us against life's dangers. The left brain is essential. But we also need our right brain to feel the kind of connection and contentment that Taylor experienced when she had her stroke. The right brain perspective helps us answer Einstein's question in the affirmative: life is ultimately on our side.

Dr. Taylor was able to connect fully with the right side of her brain accidentally through a traumatic stroke. Once she found her way to the right brain, she was able to find it again and again. But how about the rest of us? How can we access the sense of connection that comes from the right brain and dissolve the optical delusion of separation that Einstein describes? How can we remember our sense of connection and common ground with others so that it becomes our default way of living? How can we consciously choose to leave behind the chatter of the left brain when it does not serve us?

Taylor believes that each of us can learn to engage the right side of the brain more frequently and easily. One way is to participate in creative and physical activities that exercise the right brain. For Taylor, these activities include waterskiing, playing the guitar, and making stained-glass art. Each of us has our own preferred ways.

One of my favorite activities is climbing mountains, which I have had the pleasure of doing ever since I was a boy of six living in the Swiss Alps. The view from a mountaintop is breathtaking. As I gaze out, with the whole world seemingly stretched out below and the sky above, I get the feeling that I'm dropping away. My body seems to shrink in comparison with the size of the mountains all around. I appear to fade into the background—a tiny dot taking its place on the canvas of the universe, an inseparable part of a bigger picture. The optical delusion dissolves for a moment and I can glimpse with my mind's eye the scientific truth that all is interconnected. I feel infinitesimal and yet somehow infinite, humbled and uplifted all at once.

We are so used to seeing the world through the lens of our left brain—logical, critical, and full of boundaries—that this "bigger picture," this sense that everything is interconnected, may seem difficult to grasp. But it is in fact the view we are all born with. Babies in the womb and at their mother's breast naturally feel connected, having little awareness of where their body ends and their mother's body begins. As adults, we may catch glimpses of this bigger picture—in moments when we feel deep love or wonder or beauty. We each have an innate ability to connect with the life around us. All we need to do is exercise it.

Because modern life, with all its activities and distractions, conflicts and negotiations, draws far more on our left brain, it helps to have a daily practice to develop our right brain capacity. Every day we can choose to spend some time on our "inner mountaintop"—through a walk in the park, a period of sitting in silence, or a time for meditation or prayer. We can contemplate or create a piece of art, or we can listen to or play a piece of beautiful music. By engaging in such activities, Taylor writes, we are creating neural pathways back to the right side of the brain, which grow stronger every time they are used.

Then, when we happen to face a difficult conversation or negotiation, we may find it easier to access the right brain and remember our sense of connection. I recall a walk I took in Paris just before a momentous business negotiation to seek an end to an acrimonious high-stakes dispute that had cost both parties and their families much personal grief as well as millions of dollars in legal fees. At the end of my walk, by chance, I passed by a new outdoor sculpture exhibit in Place Vendôme. The statues were startling in the bright sunlight: giant silver and golden buddhas from China with great beaming smiles, obviously enjoying life to the utmost. Contemplating these glowing statues suddenly put the heated conflict in perspective and inspired me with a simple phrase to start the negotiation.

An hour later seated at lunch, when my counterpart, a distinguished banker representing the other side, asked me why I had requested the meeting, I responded: "Because life is too short! Life is too short for these mutually destructive conflicts that consume people and their families with stress, tension, and a huge loss of resources." That simple phrase, which called to mind the bigger connected picture, set a constructive tone for the successful talks that followed.

MAKE YOUR OWN HAPPINESS

In negotiation, perhaps the biggest driver of win-lose thinking is a mindset of scarcity. When people feel there isn't enough to go around, conflicts tend to break out. Whether it is a fight between different department heads in the same sales organization over their slice of the budget or a quarrel between two children over a piece of cake, the game quickly becomes win-lose. In the end, both sides often end up losing. The fight damages the working relationship between the departments so that both fall short in meeting their numbers and, in the midst of the kids' quarrel, the piece of cake falls on the floor.

In my work as a mediator, I have found that one of the most effective negotiating strategies is to look for creative ways to "expand the pie" before dividing it up. For example, the two departments could explore ways in which, through greater cooperation, they could increase sales and justify an increase in the budget for both. Or the children could find some ice cream to add to the cake so there is more for both. There may be limits to tangible resources, but there are few limits to human creativity. I have observed hundreds of negotiations in which both parties were able to create more value for each other through such creativity.

Yet, as I have noticed, it is not always easy for people to expand the pie. Sometimes, the obstacle lies in the nature of the resource; there just seems to be no way to create more value. But perhaps more often, in my experience, the obstacle lies in our mindset of scarcity, an underlying assumption that there is a "fixed pie" that cannot be expanded. How then can we reframe the picture and change our mindset from scarcity to sufficiency or even abundance? What helps, I find, is to look for ways to expand our "inner pie," which can then make it easier for us to expand the outer pie.

Harvard psychologist Daniel Gilbert likes to challenge his audiences by asking a question about happiness: "Who is likely to be happier: someone who wins millions of dollars in the lottery or someone who loses both their legs?" Everyone believes the answer is obvious—but it is not. The astonishing answer from the research is that, after a year passes, the lotto winners and the amputees are about as equally happy as they were before the event.

The research suggests that, with a few exceptions, major events or traumas that occur even three months earlier have little to no effect on our present happiness. The reason, Gilbert goes on to explain, is that we are able to make our own happiness. We change the way we see the world so that we can feel better. We are much more resilient than we imagine. "The lesson . . . ," Gilbert says, "is that our longings and our worries are both to some degree overblown because we have within us the capacity to manufacture the very commodity we are constantly chasing." As Gilbert's research suggests, we may think that happiness is something to be *pursued outside* us, but it is actually something that we *make inside.*

This conclusion may be hard to believe, particularly because many of us have been taught from early on that happiness and fulfillment come from external conditions such as money, success, or status. Julio, a successful economist, found himself at age twenty-seven having accomplished everything he had wanted. He was a manager at a multinational strategy firm. He was in a good relationship. He had moved to New York City to open up an office and complete his MBA. Julio explains:

> From the time I was young, I had this image of what success looked like: two cell phones, working all the time, traveling. And now I had achieved it. But then one day I woke up and felt a sadness and emptiness

inside. I felt incomplete. None of what I had achieved made any sense to me. None of it was going to give me the feeling of peace and calm that I wanted.

Julio went in search of what was missing: He slowed down his life a little and took up meditation. He started spending more time with himself and more time in nature. "Eventually I discovered that the peace and calm I wanted was already inside me. I just had to stop and look. And then I noticed that the changes inside me produced changes outside of me," Julio remarked. "I was less stressed at work, kinder to people, calmer. And people around me noticed. I was a better colleague, a better boss, a better employee."

Julio discovered that the outer happiness he was pursuing was fleeting and by its very nature scarce. It came, for example, after he achieved a career goal, and then it went away. Only inner contentment, the kind he could make himself, was sufficient and enduring. By taking up activities that stimulated his right brain, like time in nature and meditation, he was able to reframe his view of life, which made him a better person to be around. By getting to yes with himself, Julio found it easier to get to yes with others.

Abraham Lincoln had a point when he reflected a long time ago: "I have come to realize that people are about as happy as they make up their minds to be." Our ability to meet our deepest needs for happiness and contentment is, in fact, part of our nature. As children we know this instinctively but, as adults, we somehow cover up our essential nature with life's daily worries and instead hope that others—our spouses, our bosses, our colleagues, our friends—will meet our needs. We often end up in conflicts and difficult negotiations precisely because we believe that only the other person can make us satisfied—typically by relinquishing something he or she has and that we want.

The truth is that, to a much greater degree than we might imagine, we each have the capacity to take care of our own deeper needs for contentment. It is our birthright, a capacity that has been there all the time and that we simply need to reclaim, as Julio did. Each in our own way, we can begin to discover the simple things of life that make us happy. No matter how difficult life may seem at times, it is also capable of providing us what we need most. Life is our ally.

If, as Professor Gilbert's research suggests, we are capable of manufacturing our own happiness, then the very thing we most want, happiness, is not scarce at all, but sufficient and possibly even abundant. To a great extent, it depends on us. Could it be that we have been going thirsty while perched atop a spring of abundant flowing water?

In my work helping others get to yes, I had long made the

conventional assumption that, if I can help people obtain the *outer* satisfaction of a good agreement, it will provide the *inner* satisfaction they seek. If only they can get the other person to agree to do what they want, then they will be satisfied and happy. People are naturally disappointed when the other person refuses to say yes or to properly carry out his or her part of the bargain. I have long observed the frustration, anger, sadness, and destructive conflict that ensues and wondered if there is a better way.

Over the years, I have come to realize that my original working assumption was incorrect. The outer satisfaction of a good agreement usually only brings temporary inner satisfaction. True enduring satisfaction starts inside. From inner satisfaction comes outer satisfaction that then feeds back inner satisfaction—and so on in a virtuous circle that begins from within.

The potential benefits for our negotiations and relationships are great. Paradoxically, the less dependent we feel on others to satisfy our needs for happiness, the more mature and truly satisfying our relationships with others are likely to be. The less needy we feel, the less conflict there will be and the easier it will be for us to get to yes in challenging situations.

In my experience, moreover, people who have rediscovered their capacity to create inner satisfaction are far less likely to get trapped in a mindset of scarcity and more likely to use their innate creativity to expand the pie. Here is the point I had missed before: if you want to expand the pie in your negotiations, whether with your spouse or your work partner, your children or your boss, begin by finding ways to expand the pie inside.

APPRECIATE LIFE'S LESSONS

As my father-in-law Curt—Opa, as we called him—lay on his deathbed, succumbing to cancer, surrounded by his family, he would oscillate between moments of sheer terror and moments of profound peace. This was a man who, because of his own childhood experiences that included witnessing firsthand the firebombing of Hamburg during World War II, had definitely answered Einstein's question in the negative. In Opa's view, the world was an unfriendly place full of scarcity and danger. In a letter he wrote his sixteen-year-old grandson Chris, his principal advice about life was: "Don't trust anyone."

One day, however, a few weeks before he died, Opa announced that during the night, he had experienced a deep change in his perspective: "Here," he declared, "we believe that everything is against us. Now I can see that everything is in our favor." Although he had not known it, life had always been his ally, teaching him and helping him grow, even through challenging moments. On his deathbed, he had finally come to answer Einstein's question in the affirmative. Reframing his basic assumptions about life allowed him to finally relax and to let go of his fear and distrust. Instead of resisting the dying process, he was able to embrace it with gratitude for all he had been given in his life. His emotional suffering abated and he died a fulfilled man with his family all around him, loving him.

I used to believe that gratitude for life came from being happy, but I have come to realize that the reverse is also true, perhaps even more so: being happy comes from feeling grateful for life. There may be no better gateway to happiness than cultivating our gratitude. One of the foremost scientific researchers on gratitude, Dr. Robert A. Emmons, reports:

We've discovered scientific proof that when people regularly work on cultivating gratitude, they experience a variety of measurable benefits: psychological, physical, and social. In some cases, people have reported that gratitude led to transformative life changes. And even more importantly, the family, friends, partners, and others who surround them

consistently report that people who practice gratitude seem measurably happier and are more pleas-
ant to be around. I've concluded that gratitude is
one of the few attitudes that can measurably change
peoples' lives.

Gratitude for life does not mean denying what is painful, but being able to understand the bigger picture. Once,
while I was beginning work on this book, my daughter,
Gabi, suddenly experienced sharp pains in her abdomen
and was taken to the hospital. She was suffering greatly
from nausea and distention. For Gabi, Lizanne, and me,
those days were filled with fear, despair, and sadness. At
one low point, Lizanne and I were afraid we might be losing
our precious daughter. After four days of a worsening state
and continuing pain, and with an uncertain diagnosis, the
doctors suddenly decided to do a major emergency operation at midnight for a total obstruction of the intestine. As
it turned out, the surgery was just in time as the intestine
was minutes away from bursting.

Then, gradually over the ensuing days, Gabi slowly recovered and we felt intense relief. During that difficult time,
Lizanne, in particular, learned a powerful lesson about
acceptance and resilience that gave her renewed confidence
in her ability to handle whatever adversities might come

her way. She could either lament the unfairness of life or she could practice gratitude—gratitude for Gabi's life and her recovery and the lessons that came with it. Lizanne chose gratitude.

By feeling grateful for life, we open ourselves to the possibility of experiencing what the Viennese philosopher Ludwig von Wittgenstein called "absolute safety." Wittgenstein was speaking from his personal experiences serving in the midst of fierce battles during World War I, watching men die by the hundreds and thousands around him. By absolute safety, Wittgenstein meant "the state of mind in which one is inclined to say, 'I am safe, nothing can injure me whatever happens.'" Absolute safety, he observed, comes from a sense of gratitude and wonder at the very existence of the world. Our bodies remain frail and vulnerable, of course, but the feeling is one of absolute safety. By seeing the universe as essentially friendly even in times of danger, we can help address one of our deepest needs—the need to feel safe.

FROM UNFRIENDLY TO FRIENDLY

In *Man's Search for Meaning,* Dr. Viktor Frankl tells the story of a young woman, a patient of his, who lay desperately ill in a Nazi concentration camp:

This young woman knew that she would die in the next few days. But when I talked to her she was cheerful in spite of this knowledge. "I am grateful that fate has hit me so hard," she told me. "In my former life I was spoiled and did not take spiritual accomplishments seriously." Pointing through the window of the hut, she said, "This tree here is the only friend I have in my loneliness." Through that window she could see just one branch of a chestnut tree, and on the branch were two blossoms. "I often talk to this tree," she said to me.

I was startled and didn't quite know how to take her words. Was she delirious? Did she have occasional hallucinations? Anxiously I asked her if the tree replied. "Yes." What did it say to her? She answered, "It said to me, 'I am here—I am here—I am life, eternal life.'"

Here she was in a place of great suffering, about to die, lonely and isolated, away from all family and friends, yet astonishingly, Frankl describes this young woman as "cheerful" and "grateful" for the life lessons her hard fate had brought her. By befriending a tree, actually just a single branch with two blossoms, she found a way to connect with life in the face of imminent death. She was thus able to make her own happiness and relish her last remaining hours. Even in such dire conditions, she was able to answer Einstein's question in the affirmative and experience the universe as a friend in the form of a tree.

If we can take a lesson from the experience of a young woman whose name we will never know, it might be to remember our astonishing human capacity to reframe the picture: to remember our connection with life, to find happiness even in what may seem like small things, and to appreciate life's lessons. Life can be extremely challenging at times, but we can choose whether or not to see the challenges as being ultimately in our favor. We can choose to learn from these challenges, even the most difficult ones.

As Frankl made eloquently and poignantly clear in his book, whose original title in German was *Saying Yes to Life in Spite of Everything,* we have the power to choose our basic attitude toward life, which then directly influences our attitude toward others. Instead of saying *no* to life, seeing life as unfriendly, we can choose to say *yes* to life, seeing life as our friend. In making this fundamental choice, we are able to shape our lives, our relationships, and our negotiations for the better.

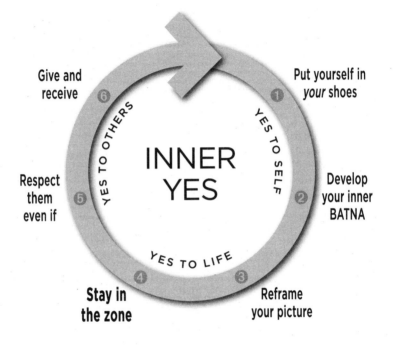

Give and receive

Put yourself in *your* shoes

Respect them even if

Develop your inner BATNA

Stay in the zone

Reframe your picture

YES TO OTHERS

YES TO SELF

YES TO LIFE

INNER YES

STAY IN THE ZONE

FROM RESISTANCE TO ACCEPTANCE

He who lives not in time, but in the present, is happy.
—LUDWIG VON WITTGENSTEIN

The pressure was on. At the invitation of the United Nations and the Carter Center, I had been working as a third party in the acute political crisis afflicting Venezuela. Millions of people were on the streets of the capital city, Caracas, calling for the downfall of President Hugo Chavez. Millions of others were on the streets supporting him. People were arming themselves, rumors were circulating about imminent attacks, and international observers were seriously concerned about the possible outbreak of a civil war.

I had received a call from former president Jimmy Carter

asking me to meet with President Chavez to discuss how to avert a serious escalation. A meeting was set and I wanted to make the most of this perhaps onetime opportunity to influence the country's leader. I was preparing the most intelligent advice I could offer. But why, I asked myself, would he even listen to me, a "yanqui professor"?

As was my habit, I went for a walk in the park to seek clarity. I suspected that I would be given only a few minutes with the president, so I was outlining in my head a brief set of recommendations to make. But what occurred to me on the walk was to do the exact *opposite* of what I had been planning: don't offer advice, unless of course requested to do so. Just listen, stay focused on the present moment, and look for openings. The risk, of course, was that the meeting would end very soon and I would lose my one chance to influence him with my advice, but I decided to take it.

When the day of the meeting came, tensions were high and protesters were agitating outside the presidential palace. When my colleague Francisco Diez and I arrived, we were asked to wait and then taken to a large ornate receiving room where we were greeted by President Chavez. He invited us to take sofa chairs beside his. I thanked him for the meeting, gave him President Carter's regards, and asked him about his four-year-old daughter, who was the same age as mine. And I let the conversation unfold naturally.

Soon Chavez was talking freely about his story. He had been a colonel in the military. He had resigned in outrage that he and his troops had been ordered to shoot to kill civilians to quell a riot over food prices in Caracas. He had subsequently launched a coup d'etat and had gone to prison. When released, he ran for president. He talked of his fervent admiration for Simon Bolivar, the liberator of Latin America from Spanish rule in the early 1800s. I listened closely, trying to understand what it was like to be in his shoes.

When he finished his story, he turned to me, and asked, "Okay, Professor Ury, what do you think of the conflict here in Venezuela?"

"Señor Presidente, I have worked as a third party in many civil wars. Once the bloodshed starts, it is very difficult to end. I believe that you have a great opportunity now to prevent a war before it happens."

"How?" he asked.

"Open up a dialogue with the opposition."

"*Negotiate* with them?" He reacted with visible anger. "They are traitors who tried to mount a coup against me and kill me less than a year ago right here in this very room!"

I paused for a moment, going to the balcony. Rather than argue with him, I decided to follow his train of thought.

"I understand. Since you can't trust them at all, what's the use of talking with them?"

"Exactly," he responded.

I was just focused on the present moment, looking for an opening, and a question occurred to me: "Since you don't trust them, understandably given what happened to you, let me ask you: What action if any could they possibly take tomorrow morning that would send you a credible signal that they were ready to change?"

"*Señales?* Signals?" he asked as he paused to consider the unexpected question.

I said yes.

"Well, for one, they could stop calling me a *mono* [monkey] on their TV stations." He gave a bitter laugh. "And they could stop putting uniformed generals on television calling for the overthrow of the government. That's treason!"

Within minutes, the president agreed to designate his minister of the interior to work with Francisco and me to develop a list of possible practical actions that each party could take to build trust and de-escalate the crisis. The president asked us to come back to meet with him the very next day to report on our progress. A constructive process for beginning to defuse the grave political crisis had unexpectedly opened up.

As Francisco and I said good-bye to President Chavez,

I glanced at my watch. I had lost track of time and a full two and a half hours had passed. I am convinced that, if I had followed my first thought to begin the meeting by reciting my recommendations, the president would have cut the meeting short after a few minutes. After all, he had a long line of people waiting to see him. Instead, because I had deliberately let go of trying to give advice and instead just stayed present and attentive to possible openings, the meeting had become highly productive.

If we want to get to yes in a sensitive situation, the key is to look for the *present opportunity,* the chance to steer the conversation toward a yes, as happened with President Chavez. In most situations, I find, there is an opening if we are attentive enough to see it. But it is all too easy for us to miss. I have been in so many negotiations where one party signals an opening or even makes a concession and the other party does not notice it. Whether it is a marital argument or a budget disagreement in the office, it is so easy for us to be distracted, to be thinking about the past or worrying about the future. Yet it is only in the present moment when we can intentionally change the direction of the conversation toward an agreement.

I learned this lesson of looking for the present opportunity many years ago from my mentor and colleague Roger Fisher. While the other university professors I knew focused on either understanding the history of a particular conflict or predicting its future, Roger focused on the present opportunity for constructive action. "*Who* can do *what* today to move this conflict toward resolution?" was the question he always liked to ask. Roger knew that, as interesting and informative as the past or future might be, the power to transform the conflict lay in the present moment. His focus on the ever-available opportunity to move toward a yes was an eye-opening lesson for me.

But what I did not fully appreciate at that time is the prior step that makes it possible for us to focus on the present opportunity in our interactions with others. If we are to spot the present opportunity, our internal focus naturally needs to be in the present moment. Our best performance comes from being in a state of relaxed alertness, paying attention to the here and now. Research psychologist Mihaly Csikszentmihalyi called this state "flow" in his celebrated book about the psychological state of high performance and inner satisfaction. Athletes sometimes call this state the "zone." If tennis players, for example, get preoccupied with their last point or the next point, they will not perform well. Being fully present—being in the zone—they can surrender to the moment and play their best. Former sprinter Mark Richardson, talking about his experience of being in the zone as a runner, explains:

It's a very strange feeling. It's as if time slows down and you see everything so clearly. You just know that everything about your technique is spot on. It just feels so effortless; it's almost as if you're floating across the track. Every muscle, every fiber, every sinew is working in complete harmony and the end product is that you run fantastically well.

Just as it is valuable for tennis players, runners, and other athletes to stay in the zone, so it is for us when we are trying to get to yes with others, whether with a spouse or partner, a work colleague, or a client. As I discovered in my meeting with President Chavez, being fully attentive in the present moment makes us less likely to react, helps us pay attention to possible openings, and accesses our natural creativity so that we can more easily reach mutually satisfying agreements. In addition to its positive effects on our performance, the "zone" is also where we tend to experience the greatest inner satisfaction and enjoyment.

It is not easy at all, however, to stay focused on the present moment. Perhaps the biggest obstacle is an internal *resistance* or *no* to life as it is: we regret the past, worry about the future, and reject our present circumstances. The key to staying in the zone is to let go of this internal resistance and accept the past, trust the future, and embrace the present, just as they are. The key, in other words, is to say *yes* to life.

LEARN TO LET GO

Relaxing our tight grip on life may be harder than it seems. I am reminded of my adventures as a mountain climber in my teens and twenties. After my friend Dusty and I had climbed up to the very top of a peak, we would descend by rappelling, using a rope to lower ourselves down the precipice. To rappel, we would walk backward off a ledge and then walk down the cliff face, sometimes over a thousand feet high, holding ourselves perpendicular to the surface. At first, it was unnerving and frightening to rappel down; every instinct in my body told me not to let go and let myself fall off the precipice. But if I did not loosen my grip on the rope, I would get stuck, unable to descend the mountain. My desire to control the situation—and fear of what might happen if I didn't—stood starkly in the way of making any progress and getting what I wanted: to get back down.

Sometimes we don't really want to let go of our controlling grip on life—just as I didn't want to let go of the rope when I first learned to rappel. We may believe that worrying incessantly about the future will keep us out of danger. We may enjoy brooding over the past, blaming others because it makes us feel righteous and superior, or more alive through the anger. We may want to control and even fight our present circumstances when they don't fit our expectations or our plans. As George Bernard Shaw once observed: "People become attached to their burdens sometimes more than the burdens are attached to them."

For all these reasons, overcoming our resistance to letting go is a slow process. To learn to rappel, I started by relaxing my grip on the rope for a few seconds, feeling that I was safe, and then loosening my grip a little more, followed by holding on again, and so on until eventually I became fully comfortable and accustomed to walking backward off a cliff. Once I did let go of the rope, there was nothing to do except to enjoy the view. We need the same mixture of patience and persistence to meet the challenge of letting go and staying in the zone. After a while, it gets easier until we don't even give it a moment's thought.

One time, I remember vividly, Dusty and I had to rappel down from a high alpine peak in a storm with pouring rain whipping into our faces amid distant claps of thunder and occasional flashes of lightning. We found ourselves on a small rock ledge and the only thing that seemed available to serve as an anchor for the rope was a small slender pine tree clinging to the cliff. In a hurry, we wrapped the rope around the tree, tugged on the tree to test it, and proceeded.

As I began to lower myself over the lip of the high precipice and entrusted my full weight to the rope, the pine tree shivered and then—as if in slow motion—came uprooted. I grasped for the edge of the ledge and caught myself just in time. Dusty and I looked at each other, speechless, shocked by what might have happened. We stopped, looked around with some diligence, and finally found a more reliable anchor, a boulder. This time we were able to rappel safely down the mountain. Needless to say, Dusty and I learned to appreciate keenly the value of anchoring ourselves to something solid before letting go.

I find that the same lesson holds true for letting go of our tight grip on life. Our ability to relax and let life flow naturally depends on how solidly anchored we feel in a friendly world. If we can reframe our picture of life and find satisfaction from within, then we will be more willing to let go of our resentments about the past and our anxieties about the future. Reframing allows us to relax and to accept life just as it is.

ACCEPT THE PAST

"When I think of what Craig has done to me, I feel furious," said one client of mine enmeshed in a business dispute to me during a moment of candor. "So it gives me pleasure to attack him. If I settle our dispute, what will my life be like without my private war?" He was so focused on the past and on the pleasure of revenge that he had lost sight of his true objectives in the negotiation and in life.

As a mediator in family feuds, labor strikes, and civil wars, I have witnessed the heavy shadow of the past and how it can create bitterness, resentment, and hatred. I have listened for days to blame and recriminations and who did what to whom. I have observed how easily the human mind gets bogged down in the past and forgets the present opportunity to end the conflict and the suffering.

Holding on to the past is not only self-destructive because it distracts us from reaching a mutually satisfying agreement, but it also takes away our joy and even harms our health. And it affects those around us who are our biggest supporters in life. Watching us hold on to the past and poison our present takes away *their* joy and well-being. It is a loss for everyone. If we truly realized how much it costs us to hold on to the past, how self-destructive it ultimately is, we might not wait so long to let go.

In the dispute above, once my client was able to let go of his temptation to dwell on the past and to settle his differences with his adversary, he told me he was a different man, feeling much lighter. Even his young children had noticed—and probably worried about—how much their father had been consumed by the conflict. When it ended, they saw, clearly relieved, a noticeable change in their father: "Daddy is not on the cell phone all the time," they told their mother.

Letting go of the past can be truly liberating. In a speech at the UN, former U.S. president Bill Clinton recalled a question he once asked Nelson Mandela: "Tell me the truth: when you were walking down the road that last time [as Mandela was released from prison], didn't you hate them?" Mandela replied: "I did. I am old enough to tell the truth. I felt hatred and fear but I said to myself, if you hate them when you get in that car, you will still be their prisoner. I wanted to be free and so I let it go."

Here was a man who had spent twenty-seven years in prison and had every reason to be bitter and angry. The great and unexpected gift he gave to his compatriots was to help them let go of the heavy burden of the past so that they could get to yes and begin to build a free South Africa for all. By learning to accept and forgive his former jailers, Mandela inspired thousands of others to forgive too. One was a young fellow prisoner at Robben Island, Vusumzi Mcongo, who had been severely tortured in detention for his role in leading a student boycott. "We cannot live with broken hearts," Mcongo said. "In time we have to accept that these things have happened to us, that those years have been wasted. To stay with the past will only bring you into turmoil."

Forgiving those who have wronged us does not mean condoning or forgetting what they did. It means accepting what happened and freeing ourselves from its weight. The first beneficiary of forgiveness, after all, is ourselves. Resentment and anger tend to consume us and hurt us perhaps much more even than they hurt the other. Holding on to old resentments makes about as much sense as carrying our bags while traveling on a train; it only tires us out needlessly.

As important as it is to forgive others, perhaps the most important person to forgive is oneself. Without doubt, at some point each of us has felt regret, guilt, shame, self-hatred, and self-blame for all the ways in which we have broken promises to ourselves and hurt ourselves as well as others. These feelings naturally tend to fester and take our attention away from the present moment. That's why the poet Maya Angelou urged that forgiving ourselves is crucial:

If you live, you will make mistakes—it is inevitable. But once you do and you see the mistake, then you forgive yourself . . . If we all hold on to the mistake, we can't see our own glory in the mirror because we have the mistake between our faces and the mirror.

Accepting the past is not only about letting go of accusations toward others and ourselves; it's also about accepting the experiences life has given us, however challenging these might be. If we don't let go of our resentment and regret, we become prisoners of the past. To accept our past, it helps to reframe our stories and give a positive meaning to even the most difficult life events. We may have no power to change the past, but we do have the power to change the meaning we assign to it.

If I did not believe before in the power of reframing our stories, certainly the experience with my daughter Gabi's medical challenges has persuaded me of it. In the early years after Gabi's birth, my wife, Lizanne, told me she felt she was in a dark tunnel out of which she would never emerge. But over time she and I learned to paint a different picture of the experience. The truth was that, as painful and difficult as it was to watch our daughter undergo medical procedure after medical procedure, it challenged Lizanne and me to grow as human beings and to draw on our inner resources. We can only be grateful for the valuable life lessons Gabi's journey brought to us—lessons reflected in this book. I personally deepened my ability to observe my thoughts and feelings, to put myself in my shoes, to see life as an ally and friend. Looking back, Lizanne and I have come to appreciate the entire experience as a "blessed shock," one that paradoxically woke us up to life's potential for experiencing joy in the present. While we would not have voluntarily chosen this path, I can say without a doubt that each of us is happier and more fulfilled today because of all we learned as a result. In fact, I do not believe I would be writing this book were it not for these experiences.

TRUST THE FUTURE

Once when I was speaking to a group of businesspeople about the critical importance of developing your BATNA—your Best Alternative To a Negotiated Agreement—a man came up to me and said, "Yes, that's true. But I also like to think about my WATNA—my *Worst* Alternative To a Negotiated Agreement."

"Why is that?" I asked, my curiosity piqued.

"Because I worry a lot about what's going to happen if things go wrong in the negotiation," he replied. "It helps me to think about the worst thing that could happen because then I can say to myself: 'If they're not going to kill me, then I will probably survive.' And I laugh it off."

There is a lot of truth in that man's comment. We do tend to worry a lot in negotiation and in life, in general, about all the bad things that could happen. While keeping an eye on the future can be useful, worrying about it continually only takes us away from the present moment so that we no longer operate at our best.

I am well acquainted with fear from my work in dangerous conflicts. I have often watched fear take hold of me and of others. But what I've learned over the years is that the vast majority of our fears are baseless. As the French philosopher Michel de Montaigne noted four centuries ago: "My life has been full of terrible misfortunes most of which never happened." In the end, fear ends up doing more damage to us than the very danger it imagines. "He who fears he shall suffer," Montaigne concluded, "already suffers what he fears."

The alternative to fear is trust. By trust, I don't mean the belief that there will be no challenges or painful experiences. Rather, I mean the confidence that you will be able to deal with the challenges that come your way. That trust is what enabled me to have the productive conversation with President Chavez described at the beginning of this chapter. If I had listened to my fear of failure, I would never have let the conversation flow naturally into what became a real opening in the negotiation.

Trust is not a onetime shift in attitude, but rather a conscious choice we face many times a day. In every interaction with others, a client or a boss, a spouse or partner, we can choose between fear and trust. Will we obey the *no* voice that counsels us not to look foolish or ridiculous? Or will we listen to the *yes* voice that encourages us to take a chance and follow our intuition?

Winston Churchill once quipped, "The pessimist sees the difficulty in every opportunity. The optimist sees the opportunity in every difficulty." He went on to say, "I am an optimist. It does not seem much use being anything else." Trust in the future, as he knew well from the horrors of war, does not mean ignoring life's problems. On the contrary, trust is an attitude with which we can actively deal with our problems. Why not try out this attitude and see if trusting— that you can handle whatever life brings you—works better for you than continually worrying about the future?

A number of practical methods can help us let go of our fear of the future. You can observe the fear when it shows up and then consciously release it, shaking it off a bit like a dog shakes off the water after plunging into a lake. You can take a deep breath or two, bringing oxygen into your brain so you can see things more clearly. Or like the businessman I cited earlier, you can also ask yourself a simple but powerful reality-testing question when you are anxious about a particular future outcome: *What is the worst thing that can happen here?* By facing your fears from a place of clarity, you'll be better able to relax and to stay in the zone. Our bodies do not distinguish between real threats and imagined threats as they gear up for fight or flight, so in the great majority of situations, a little bit of perspective can go a long way in helping us let go of fear.

In the end, perhaps the surest way to free yourself from unnecessary fears is to remember your inner BATNA and your *yes* to life. Your commitment to take care of your needs and your confidence that life is on your side will give you a sense that, no matter what happens in the future, everything will be okay in the end.

An old Chinese proverb counsels: "That the birds of worry and care fly over your head, this you cannot change, but that they build nests in your hair, this you can prevent."

EMBRACE THE PRESENT

Once we release ourselves from the burden of the past and from the shadow of the future, then we are freer to live and act in the present. We can visit the past from time to time to learn from it and we can visit the future to plan and take necessary precautions, but we make our home in the only place where we can make positive change happen: in the present moment. It is by being present and spotting the present opportunities in our negotiations that we can most easily get to yes with others.

It is all too easy in today's world of cell phones, texts, and e-mail to get distracted from the present moment. Underlying our tendency to distract ourselves is a resistance to the way that life is for us right now. We tend to have idealized expectations of how life *should* or *should not* be, and our inner judge is constantly comparing our reality to that expectation. We keep score. "I *should* have made the sale by now." "I *should not* have just spoken that way to my boss." "My spouse *should* be nicer to me." A telltale sign of expectations are the words *should* and *should not*.

Accepting life as it is does not mean resigning ourselves to the way things are. In fact, constructive change starts from accepting reality regardless of how painful it might be—not from losing time and energy resisting it. My friend Judith had a very difficult time when her son Ben went through a phase of rebellion that had started when he was nine and reached a peak of intensity when he was thirteen. Ben would repeatedly—and harshly—reject her and her attempts to connect with him. Judith was on a roller coaster of hurt and anger, helplessness and determination, grief and tears. She felt as though she was falling apart.

"I would not let go. I felt like I was fighting for my life and for that of my son," Judith explained. "My husband was running up and down the stairs to the basement family room where Ben had moved, like a frantic mediator attempting to carry messages between the rebel forces and the crumbling government."

Judith was expressing a loud *no* to Ben's behavior, essentially a *no* to life as it showed up in the present moment. No matter how much she struggled and resisted, however, she was unable to force Ben to accept her at that point. It is not easy to let go of trying to control life, particularly when the stakes seem high.

Behind our fear of letting go may be the false assumption that if we don't control all the circumstances around us, then everything will fall apart and our lives will be destroyed. Our instinct is to protect our idealized version of how life ought to be. The irony, of course, is that resisting our present reality is destructive not only to us, but also to those around us. In Judith's case, her relationship with her husband was severely strained by their mutual judgment, blame, hurt, and helplessness.

So how do we, in fact, let go?

Judith learned to let go by testing her assumptions about the future, which motivated much of her need to control her relationship with her son. One day, while walking on the trail behind her home, she asked herself: *What is the worst thing that could happen here?* "Other than my child dying," Judith realized, "the worst thing I could imagine was that I would end up having active relationships with only two of my three children." In negotiation terms, she was asking herself a reality-testing question, a question about her best alternative if she was not able to get to yes with her son.

Suddenly Judith's situation didn't seem so dire. She asked herself: *Can I live with this? Can I be happy even if I never have a good relationship with my son?* And the answer was clear—she could. "It wasn't what I wanted," Judith clarifies, "but I could live with it. I still had the capacity to find joy and satisfaction in my life. My well-being was not dependent on this child's love or approval." In that brief moment, Judith felt liberated from the tyranny of her fears.

"Gradually, I *let go*," Judith explains. "I let go of needing his acknowledgment, of needing him to love me or even needing him to like me. I let go of needing him to call or talk to me. I let go of needing him to feel the same way about me as he did about his father. And ultimately, I let go of needing any relationship with him at all. As I faced my life as it was, rather than life as I had hoped it would be, my pictures of myself as a mother, a wife, of being anyone I had previously thought I was, fell away. In place of this came freedom."

Once Judith was able to let go of her expectations of how life should be, then paradoxically healthy change unfolded—naturally. Letting go turned out to be the unexpected key to transforming the conflict between mother and son, a relationship that healed slowly over the years. Precisely because Judith was able to let go of her neediness and accept her son just as he was, he was able after some time to come closer to her, apologize for hurting her, and tell her how much he loved her. By choosing to face life as it was, by getting to yes with herself, she was able to get to yes with her son as well as with her husband.

As Judith's case shows, it is hard to get to a mutually acceptable solution to a conflict if we have not first accepted the situation as it is. Accepting the present, I have learned, means accepting a gift from life. The present moment, as much as we might feel aversion to it—as Judith felt aversion to her contentious relationship with her son—is indeed a present. We might imagine that we were supposed to get another gift, but the present is what it is.

In this matter, perhaps my greatest teacher is my daughter, Gabi. Here she is, having undergone fourteen major surgeries, yet she doesn't lose any time looking back with resentment or regret or feeling sorry for herself. She shakes it off. She has a zest for life and finds enjoyment and excitement every day. If I find my mind wandering to her past or worrying about her future, I simply remember her laser-like focus on the present—and I let go. If she can relax and stay in the zone, then I can do the same.

As Lizanne and I learned from watching Gabi go through so many surgeries, pain happens. It is part of life. But when we resist life and its pain, we start to suffer. As the saying goes, pain may be inevitable but suffering is optional. We may think that it is the suffering that causes us to resist, but paradoxically it is the resistance that causes us to suffer. We get trapped in disappointment and endless wishing that this was not happening to us. Resisting our current circumstances often prolongs the misery, sometimes indefinitely. It is not easy, of course, but we can choose to limit our suffering through gradually learning to let go of our *no*—our resistance— and saying *yes*—learning to accept life as it is.

If there is a single lesson I have learned, it is this: in life, we are destined to lose many things. That is the nature of life. Never mind. Just don't lose the present. Nothing is worth it. There is nothing more important than "this," the fullness of life right now.

A key to staying in the present moment, I have learned, is to be able to focus on what lasts while accepting what passes. It is to stay anchored in our essential connection to life while we say yes to situations that pass us by—some good, some painful. Let the passing pass, let the lasting last. By focusing on what is lasting—life itself, nature, the universe—we become more aware of what is passing, more appreciative of the preciousness and temporary nature of every experience. In turn, as we become more aware that these experiences won't last forever, we become less reactive in situations of conflict—after all, whatever the conflict is, this too shall pass—and we find it easier to look for the present opportunity to get to yes with others.

FROM RESISTANCE TO ACCEPTANCE

If the first step in saying *yes* to life is to reframe our picture of life as friendly, the second step is to stay in the zone—a place of high performance and satisfaction. Accepting life means saying *yes* to the past, letting go of lingering resentments and grievances. It means saying *yes* to the future, letting go of needless worries and replacing fear with trust. And it means saying *yes* to the present, letting go of our expectations and appreciating what we have in the moment. It is not always easy, of course. It takes strength to forgive the past, courage to trust the future, and disciplined focus to stay present in the midst of life's constant problems and distractions. But, however great the challenge, the rewards of inner contentment, satisfying agreements, and healthy relationships are much greater.

Having examined our attitude toward life, it is time to examine our attitude toward others. Saying *yes* to life prepares us for the next challenge, which is to say *yes* to others.

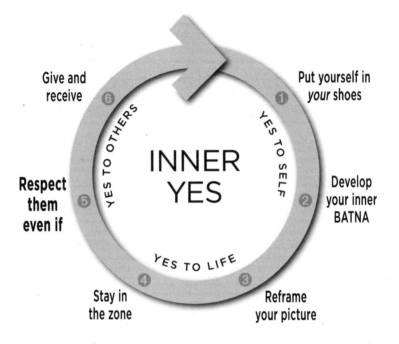

Give and receive ⑥

Put yourself in *your* shoes ①

YES TO OTHERS

YES TO SELF

INNER YES

Respect them even if ⑤

Develop your inner BATNA ②

YES TO LIFE

Stay in the zone ④

Reframe your picture ③

5

RESPECT THEM EVEN IF

FROM EXCLUSION TO INCLUSION

He drew a circle that shut me out—
Heretic, rebel, a thing to flout.
But love and I had the wit to win:
We drew a circle that took him in!

—EDWIN MARKHAM

The atmosphere was tense. There were sixty people in the room, forty from management and twenty from the union about to start a labor contract negotiation. Relations had been strained for decades with many protracted strikes and court fights. This time around promised to be no different. "Let's be clear. We are only here because the law requires it," the chief representative from management began. "We don't trust you and we don't like what you are doing." His tone was cold, antagonistic, and demeaning. On the other side of the table, the union representatives were boiling with rage.

Dennis Williams, the union leader, felt like counterattacking, but instead he controlled his temper and replied in a calm and respectful tone: "I hear you and I will tell you why *we* are here. We're here to see if we can work with you so that together we can do the best for your employees, the tens of thousands of people who make your business successful."

As Dennis told me some years later:

Even though I felt hotter than hell and my instinct was to fire back, I realized it would get us nowhere. My people were mad at me for not firing back, but eventually they understood we had to take this approach. And I can tell you, that one opening response set the tone for the rest of the negotiation. Later many people from the other side came up to me and told me that they appreciated what I had said. That little bit of respect really changed the course of how the negotiation went. It was one of only three times in over sixty years that we succeeded in reaching agreement on a contract without a big fight.

In my negotiation experience, I've long noticed that the cheapest concession you can make, the one that costs you the least and yields the most, is to give respect. To respect simply means to give positive attention and to treat the other with the dignity with which you would like to be treated. The word *respect* comes from Latin roots that mean "re" as in *repeat* and "spect" as in *spectacles*. In this sense, respect means to "look again." It is to see the other person with new eyes as a human being worthy of positive regard. If we want to get to yes with others, there can be no more important way to begin than to give them basic human respect.

Yet, as beneficial as it can be, giving respect is often a difficult concession for people to make. In a problematic situation or relationship, respect may be the last thing we feel like giving. We may think that they do not *deserve* our respect and that they need to earn it. They may not be respecting us, so why should we respect them? If we feel rejected, as the union leader did, we naturally reject back. If we feel excluded, we naturally exclude back. If we feel attacked, we attack back. Out of pain, we cause pain. It is a mutually destructive cycle that has no end as I have witnessed countless times from families to businesses to communities to entire societies. The usual results are losses all around.

But, as the story of the tense negotiation between union and management suggests, it often only takes one person to change his or her attitude toward the other—from antagonism and rejection to respect—in order to change the tone and outcome of a difficult conversation. That person could be us. Once we show respect to the other party, he or she is more likely to show us respect. Respect can breed respect, inclusion can lead to inclusion, and acceptance can foster acceptance. Just as the union leader did, we can reverse the destructive cycle and make it a constructive one.

To offer respect, we don't need to approve of the other person's behavior, nor do we need to like that individual. We just need to make the conscious choice to treat each person with the dignity that is every human being's birthright, as difficult as this may be for us. Respect shows up as a *behavior* but it originates inside of us as an *attitude*. Respect is essentially a *yes* to others, not to their demands, but rather to their basic humanity. In this sense, respect is indivisible. When we give respect to others, we are honoring the very same humanity that exists in us. When we acknowledge the dignity of others, we are acknowledging our own dignity. We cannot truly respect others without respecting ourselves at the same time.

So how in difficult situations do we change our internal attitude from antagonism to respect? It is a natural process that cannot be forced, only nurtured. Indeed, an attitude of respect begins to emerge organically from within in the process of getting to yes with ourselves: if we have already given ourselves respect through putting ourselves in our shoes, we will find it much easier to respect others. If we have chosen to take responsibility for our lives and actions, we are not likely to blame others. If we say yes to life, we will tend naturally to extend respect to others.

Still it can be difficult to give our respect, particularly in conflicts. Three specific actions can help you strengthen your attitude of respect: Put yourself in the other person's shoes. Expand your circle of respect. And, as the opening poem suggests, respect even those who at first may reject you.

PUT YOURSELF IN THEIR SHOES

While I was writing this book, I spent some days on the Turkish-Syrian border helping to conduct intensive interviews with Syrian rebel leaders in order to explore possible openings for an end to the raging civil war. My colleagues and I began by asking each leader how and why they got involved in the fight. It was one thing to read or see the news, but dramatically different to hear the tales firsthand from people living the story.

These leaders had once been pediatricians, dentists, lawyers, businesspeople, and students. Almost to a person, they had begun with peaceful protest and had suffered horrendous torture at the hands of the security services. Many of their loved ones had been killed, in some cases as recently as the day before we interviewed them. They were literally stepping out of a hellish experience in order to speak with us, and then going immediately back into the hell of war. The emotions were palpable in the air. My colleagues and I found ourselves moved and shaken as we imagined ourselves in the place of those to whom we were listening. To a greater extent than any of us had anticipated, we were feeling the others' sorrow.

Our last interview was with a young heavyset bearded man in his late twenties, a Muslim of ultraconservative Salafi belief, the commander of three thousand fighters. He looked like the Western stereotype of a fundamentalist terrorist. But any preconceptions we might have had changed as we listened to his story. We asked him how he had joined the fight. "I was in university," he replied.

"What were you studying?"

"Poetry." The young man, who came from a family of poets, had won first prize for his poetry in a national contest. When he was seventeen, he had been arrested for writing a poem that the security services found subversive. Jailed and tortured on three occasions, he joined the fight after his fellow peaceful protesters were slaughtered. He was in love with a young woman in Egypt whom he was wistfully hoping to see again if he survived.

When we asked him what his biggest concern was if his side won, we were surprised to hear him say it was religious extremism. While he believed that Islamic Sharia law was a good thing, he did not believe it should be imposed on anyone. "I'm not going to pull a gun and force my views on anyone." When at the end of the interview I asked if he had any message he would like us to convey back in our own countries, he said: "Yes, as people watch this conflict from afar, they may think we are just numbers. Please put yourself here and imagine that your child or wife is one of the numbers. Every single number has a life and a soul."

It was yet another confirmation for me of the wisdom of setting prejudgment aside and, instead, putting myself in the place of another person with dreams, loves, and grief. In the words of the poet H. W. Longfellow, "If we could read the secret history of our enemies, we should find in each man's life sorrow and suffering enough to disarm all hostility." Perhaps the easiest way to change our attitude from antagonism to respect is to put ourselves in the shoes of other people.

To show respect for those we interviewed, we set aside three hours for each interview so that the leaders would have ample time to tell their stories and feel heard. And the gesture was noticed. A number of our interviewees told us, "You are the first ones to come from abroad and actually listen to us." In that atmosphere of mutual respect, not only did we come to understand the conflict better, but we also laid the groundwork for future work on a Syrian-led solution for the Syrian conflict.

The best way to listen to others is to bring an attitude of respect, in other words, full positive attention and regard. Typically, I have observed in my negotiation work, we listen to others from within *our* frame of reference, judging what they say from our point of view. With an attitude of genuine respect, we can practice the art of listening to others from within *their* frame of reference, from their own points of view. We can listen not just to the words, but also to the feelings and unspoken thoughts that lie behind the words. We can listen not just to the content of what is being said, but also to the human being behind the content.

In my negotiation experience, I find that the simple act of imagining myself in the shoes of another person is a more powerful tool than it may seem. What does the world look like through that individual's eyes? What does it feel like to be that person? If I had lived his or her life, how would I act and react? I may not be wholly accurate in my understanding of the other person, but it never ceases to surprise me just how accurate I, or indeed anyone, often can be, simply by dint of sharing a common humanity. Our ability to empathize is a talent that is vastly underused. And, if we truly understand the other person and what he or she wants, it will naturally be a lot easier to reach agreement with that person.

Paradoxically, if we wish to become more aware of others and their concerns, there is perhaps no better work we can do than developing self-awareness. Consider the findings of a team of psychologists led by Professor David DeSteno, who recruited thirty-nine people from the Boston area for an unusual experiment. Twenty people were assigned to take a weekly meditation class for eight weeks and then to practice at home, while the remaining nineteen were informed that they were on a waiting list.

At the end of the eight-week period, the participants were invited, one by one, to come to the lab for an experiment. As each participant entered the waiting area, he or she found three chairs, two of them already occupied. As the participant took a seat and waited, a fourth person entered the room on crutches, wearing a boot for a broken foot, sighing audibly in pain as she leaned uncomfortably against the wall. Neither of the other two sitting people, who worked for the experimenters, gave up their seats. Researchers wanted to find out whether the participants in the experiment would give up their chair to the injured patient or not.

The results: 50 percent of those who had practiced meditation gave up their chair, compared to 16 percent of those who hadn't meditated—a threefold difference! DeSteno explains this dramatic difference by pointing to the documented ability of meditation to enhance attention—our ability to see others—as well as to foster a view that all beings are connected. "The increased compassion of meditators, then, might stem directly from meditation's ability to dissolve the artificial social distinctions—ethnicity, religion, ideology and the like—that divide us," DeSteno writes. It all comes down then to elementary respect—the ability to *see* another human being. Having given ourselves a "second look" through meditation, we are better able to give others a second look too.

The paradox reflected in this research is striking. By paying attention *inside* themselves through the practice of meditation, people were better able to pay attention *outside* themselves by showing kindness. *The deeper we go inside ourselves, the farther we can go outside.*

EXPAND YOUR CIRCLE OF RESPECT

Larry married a Mexican American woman and became the first non-Hispanic in her family, which provoked unspoken tensions among her in-laws, particularly with his brother-in-law Jose. Ten years later, Jose called Larry up to invite him out for a drink. After some small talk, Jose took a deep breath and went straight to the point. "He apologized," Larry remembers. "He said that he hadn't wanted an Anglo in the family. He'd lobbied behind the scenes to get his sister to break up with me. He said he'd felt bad about it for all these years. He decided it was finally time to make it right." Jose changed his attitude toward Larry from rejection to respect. He finally accepted Larry in his family and in the process resolved years of felt but unspoken conflict.

We have all probably felt rejected and excluded at some point in our lives. As children, we've felt the pain of being ignored or left out by our parents, teased or bullied by classmates, or even just picked last for games in gym class. As adults, we've all probably felt anger at being excluded, whether it is being left out of an important meeting by a boss or forgotten from an invitation to get together after work with colleagues, or simply having our ideas or needs ignored by fellow members of groups we belong to—book clubs, volunteer organizations, school meetings, you name it.

More seriously, we may get excluded from opportunities, denied rights or privileges, or treated dismissively by others or even society at large because of the color of our skin or our physical appearance, our gender or sexual preference, our nationality or ethnic heritage, or our religion, or a host of other reasons. Feeling excluded, seeing our interests and voices and basic humanity ignored, can leave deep wounds.

These painful feelings of exclusion are at the core of the great majority of the conflicts I have witnessed in my work. Israelis and Palestinians, Irish Protestants and Catholics, Serbs and Croats—I have listened at length to their stories of feeling discriminated against and humiliated, stories that often go back many generations or even centuries. These feelings fuel conflict and often trigger acts of violence. In business, I have also seen relationships break down and conflicts break out because of perceived slights such as excluding a key business partner from an important corporate meeting. And, of course, family feuds are frequently fed by feelings of being treated as less than another family member: Why did the father pick the younger brother to run the family business rather than the older brother, or the sister rather than the brother?

The only remedy I know for the wound of rejection and exclusion is the balm of recognition and acceptance—in other words, inclusion. Whether it is a family feud or an ethnic conflict or workplace tension, the way we can begin to resolve the conflict is to change our attitude and consciously expand our circle of respect to encompass others whom at first we might not want or think to include.

While I was writing this chapter, I had the chance to walk the floor of a large factory that had experienced a lot of strife and to interview workers about how they felt under the new ownership of a company called Barry-Wehmiller. Big machines were whirring away noisily. One worker tending a large machine stepped away for a moment to speak, taking off his goggles and protective earmuffs. I asked him if he had felt any difference since the change in ownership. "Yup," he replied. "The difference is that they *listen* to us." That was the essence of the change. The previous management had treated employees pretty much as paid automatons and excluded them from key decisions. The new management made real and sustained efforts to recognize them as human beings with dignity and talent and to welcome their ideas and suggestions for improving the factory. Each employee was treated as if he or she mattered, with respect.

The new attitude from management was not just talk but was reflected in their actions. Many workers at the plant recalled their experience in the midst of the 2008 financial crisis, when companies, including their competitors, were laying off employees to cut costs. The workers had expected a layoff as the previous owners had resorted to layoffs many times before. But this time, to their surprise, the CEO Robert Chapman suggested that everyone from the top down take a six-week unpaid leave so that no one would need to be laid off. It was a telling example of the principle of inclusion and the recognition of the importance of all employees and their families. Before and after the financial crisis, many factories like this one had shut down under the pressure of global competition and clashes between labor and management. Both employees and management attributed the turnaround in the business in good measure to the new attitude of respect, which inspired people to perform at their best.

Few political leaders have developed the ability to expand their circle of respect more than Abraham Lincoln. A man of great heart, he had the tragic responsibility of leading the United States during its darkest hour, the devastating and fratricidal Civil War. During the waning months of the war, Lincoln spoke publicly about the need to bind the wounds of the nation and to treat the defeated South with generosity. On one occasion in the White House when Lincoln was speaking sympathetically of the plight of the South, a Yankee patriot took him to task. "Mr. President," she decried, "how dare you speak kindly of our enemies when you ought to be thinking of destroying them?" Lincoln paused and addressed the angry patriot: "Madam," he asked, "do I not destroy my enemies when I turn them into my friends?"

Taking a lesson from Lincoln, we might look around and ask ourselves if there are any "enemies" in our lives whom we can "destroy" by turning them into our friends.

RESPECT THEM EVEN IF THEY REJECT YOU

What if the person on the other side of the table rejects us, as happens so often in conflict situations? When we feel rejected—our point of view dismissed or attacked, our needs and interests ignored—our every instinct is to protect ourselves: to pull back and reject back. It is only human to build defensive walls around ourselves if we feel attacked. Yet, when we counterattack with more rejection and disrespect, we only perpetuate the destructive cycle and render agreement impossible.

My friend Landrum Bolling, a noted peacemaker, remembers how, as a boy in school in Tennessee in the 1930s, he heard the well-known poet Edwin Markham, with a shock of white hair, declaim the poem that begins this chapter. The poet dramatically drew with his finger in the air the circle that shut him out—and then, equally dramatically, drew a much larger circle that took the other person in. That is the radical contrarian response to being excluded by others. It is a form of psychological jujitsu. In the face of rejection, do the opposite of what you at first feel like doing. Instead of rejecting others, surprise them with respect. Take the lead and change the cycle of mutual rejection into a cycle of mutual respect. That is what the union leader did in the opening story of this chapter.

Few situations are as challenging as hostage negotiations. I have had the opportunity to learn from and train police hostage negotiators, professionals who confront situations on a daily basis in big cities where people have been taken hostage, whether by bank robbers or emotionally distraught individuals. Police SWAT teams surround the place where the hostage is being held. All the weapons are drawn and everyone is on edge ready to fire. A generation ago, the standard next step was to pull out a bullhorn and shout: "You've got three minutes to come out with your hands up!" When the deadline elapsed, in would go the SWAT team with tear gas and guns. As often as not, someone was hurt or dead—the hostage, the hostage taker, or a member of the SWAT team, or all three.

Today, the police forces of major cities where hostage

incidents happen regularly have adopted a wholly different approach. Now when a hostage is taken, a professional hostage negotiation team is called in to deal with the crisis alongside the SWAT team. What is their first rule? Be polite. Give the hostage taker a hearing. Listen with close attention and acknowledge his or her point of view. Don't react, even if, as often happens, the hostage taker goes on the verbal attack. Stay cool and courteous, patient and persistent. In other words, respect and accept the very person who is attacking and rejecting. Meet exclusion with inclusion.

In the overwhelming majority of these hostage situations, the strategy of treating hostage takers with basic human respect works. It gives the hostage takers a face-saving way out. The process may take many hours, but in the end, the hostage taker usually surrenders and the hostages go free and unharmed. The parties get to yes.

As the hostage negotiators demonstrate, accepting people who reject or attack us doesn't mean ignoring injustice or evil, but rather giving respect to their humanity even as we confront their wrongful actions. Accepting those who reject us doesn't mean saying *yes* to their demands; as the hostage negotiators show, it can often mean saying *no*, but in a *positive* manner that acknowledges the other person's inherent dignity. Even where we may draw clear limits for the sake of protecting ourselves and others, accepting those who reject us means treating them as human beings just like ourselves.

It can be difficult to extend our respect to those who attack us or attack those we care about, but it is possible. I think of the story of Azim Khamisa, an American businessman I once had the privilege to meet, whose twenty-year-old son, Tariq, was killed by a young gang member. Studying during the day, Tariq worked at night delivering pizzas. One night, he came to the door of an apartment and was met by a fourteen-year-old boy named Tony who took the pizza and shot Tariq. It was a gang initiation. "When I got the phone call saying that Tariq was dead, I kind of left my body, because the pain was too much to bear," Azim said in an interview describing how he felt when he heard the news. "It was like a nuclear bomb going off inside my heart. . . . For the next few weeks I survived through prayer and was quickly given the blessing of forgiveness, reaching the conclusion there were victims at both ends of the gun."

Victims at both ends of the gun—that was Azim's astonishing and compassionate insight about his son's tragic death. Through prayer, he began to let go of the dark feelings and painful thoughts that threatened to sweep his sanity away. He was able to reframe the situation and come to see Tony through new eyes. By putting himself in the shoes of his own son's killer, he was able to forgive him— although not to forget.

Azim reached out to Tony's grandfather and guardian, Ples Felix. Deeply moved by Azim's gesture, Ples accepted Azim's offer of forgiveness. "I urged Tony to take responsibility for his actions; to minimize the pain and harm he'd done to the Khamisa family," Ples explained. "He broke down and cried. 'I'm so sorry, Daddy,' he sobbed. I held him and tried to console him. The next day everyone was expecting a plea of 'not guilty,' but Tony gave a very remorseful and emotional speech in which he pleaded guilty and asked for Mr. Khamisa's forgiveness."

Azim's courageous choice to forgive opened the possibility for Tony, the young perpetrator, to take responsibility for his actions and feel the pain of guilt and remorse rather than numb it. Azim's healing process deepened as it spread to include Tony and Ples too. Together Azim and Ples began to give talks in schools to encourage students to stop using violence against each other. They formed a foundation to advance the cause of nonviolence in schools. Azim was invited to speak around the nation, including at the White House. Five years after the killing, Azim visited Tony in jail and invited him to work at the foundation after his release. Tony told his grandfather Ples, "That is a very special man. I shot and killed his one and only son and yet he can sit with me, encourage me, and then offer me a job."

Azim's remarkable story offers us some clues about how to change our attitude from rejection to respect. Even when faced with an extreme violation, the murder of his child, Azim chose not to pursue the path of revenge but to respond by respecting Tony, his son's murderer, as a human being. Without condoning the crime in any way, he chose to forgive Tony and to include both him and his grandfather in a common effort to stop the youth violence that had claimed his son's life. Azim found a new mission in life and a deep sense of personal fulfillment. When I met him, he was on fire, an alive and contented man. Just as in the opening poem, Azim drew a larger circle and took them in.

If this strategy of meeting rejection with respect can be applied in more extreme situations like hostage taking or tragedies like Azim's, it is far easier to consider in ordinary daily situations. The next time your boss or your spouse or a colleague says or does something that makes you feel rejected and you feel the natural impulse to react, try going to the balcony instead to observe your feelings and thoughts. Put yourself in your own shoes and remember your inner BATNA, your commitment to take care of your deepest needs. If you feel more confident in your ability to make your own happiness, you will be less reactive to the other person's offensive behavior. Having given yourself respect, it will be easier for you to give others respect and to accept them even if at first they reject you. It is not easy, of course, but with practice and courage you can often turn the cycle of mutual rejection into mutual respect.

FROM EXCLUSION TO INCLUSION

The Abraham Path is a path of cultural tourism in the Middle East that retraces the ancient footsteps of Abraham, who is revered as a forefather by over half of humanity—including Christians, Muslims, and Jews. Helping to re-create the Abraham Path has been one of my great passions. On the inaugural journey, I traveled with twenty-three companions by bus across five countries, all the way from Harran in northern Mesopotamia, where Abraham set off on *his* journey four thousand years ago, to Hebron in the heart of the West Bank, where he is buried. At Harvard, my colleagues and I had been studying for years the possibility of re-creating this ancient trail as a way to inspire greater understanding among clashing cultures and faiths around the world. We encountered a lot of skepticism from those who said it would be impossible to traverse this region of roiling conflict, but we were determined to show the world that it could be done.

After twelve days of travel by bus, stopping here and there to visit places associated with Abraham and to consult with local civil, religious, and political leaders about the possibility of reestablishing this ancient path as a long-distance walking trail, we crossed the Jordan River and arrived in the city of Bethlehem in the Palestinian West Bank. The atmosphere was tense, as it happened to be the second anniversary of the death of Palestinian president Yasser Arafat. Demonstrations were expected—and who knew what else?

We visited the ancient church that sits atop the traditional birthplace of Jesus and then walked across the street to the Peace Center in Manger Square. There we sat down around a huge rectangular table for a meeting with forty or so Palestinian leaders from nonprofits, religious institutions, and government departments to present the Abraham Path project and to listen to their feedback. The minister of tourism was present as were the governor of Hebron, the chief justice of Palestine, and the imam of the Ibrahimi Mosque, the site of Abraham's traditional burial place.

My colleague Elias opened the meeting with some remarks and then turned to me to present the project. Afterward, we opened the floor for questions and suggestions from our Palestinian colleagues, giving each a chance to speak and reserving our response for the very end. While some of their comments were positive, others were cautious and critical, and still others were suspicious and hostile, even aggressive.

"The idea is unclear and ambiguous," declared one leader. "What is the Global Negotiation Project that incubated this? Who is behind this project? Does it have any links with foreign intelligence agencies or governments?" As he brought up the question of intelligence agencies, gunshots could be heard in the square outside. I could feel a tremor of nervousness pass through the room.

Then another leader spoke up: "I call on the initiators to respond to the heartbeat of the Palestinian street. We fear conspiracies based on our experience. Who is participating? What is the Israeli role?" And yet another: "How many Palestinians will be on the board? You must take a clear political stand for Palestine. For us, peace is a life and death issue." The level of tension in the room escalated as each speaker sought to outdo the previous one in being tough. Finally, after two hours of often harshly critical comments, all eyes turned back to us, and Elias asked me to respond.

I didn't know quite what to say. Under attack, I had started questioning myself: *Was the Abraham Path just a pipe dream, born from naive outsiders, destined to fail like so many other well-intentioned projects?* I felt this cherished dream of mine beginning to slip away as it was exposed to hard cold reality. But then I managed to go to the balcony, observe my thoughts and feelings, reassure myself that all was okay, and turn to the challenge facing me. Many skeptical questions had been raised, hard conditions set, and red lines drawn. How could I diminish the distrust and win the support of the critics while still keeping the project strictly nonpolitical? I realized that, if I tried to address each of their issues judiciously, I would appear defensive and only increase their suspicions. No matter what I could say, it would not be enough to satisfy them.

I tried to look at the skeptical leaders with new eyes, putting myself in their shoes. Underneath the suspicious and critical comments, I was hearing the wound of exclusion, understandably strong for people in their circumstances. The only remedy I knew for that wound was inclusion. I decided there was only one thing I could do: to step to their side.

"I am grateful for your comments. Friends are those who tell you the truth, even if it is hard to hear," I told the group of Palestinian leaders. "I understand your distrust—it is born through painful experience. You are right to have these questions and concerns. Here is the key point: you refer to us as the leaders of the project but that is not how we see

ourselves. Yes, we have been studying the social and economic potential of this path. The true leaders, however, can
only be the peoples in the region and here in this place the
leaders must be Palestinians. We can study the possibilities
and we can lend our support to overcome obstacles, but the
leadership role belongs to you. And there is no rush. *We
can wait* until you tell us you are ready. Tell us what *you*
would like to do."

Instead of rejecting their criticism or defending the project, I accepted their concerns and invited them to take the
lead. It was a calculated risk of course—the project could
have ended there—but it was a risk I felt it was necessary
to take.

The atmosphere shifted perceptibly. Suddenly the ball
was in their court. They began to talk among themselves
about what to do. One pronounced it a good thing for the
people of Palestine. Gradually they began to take ownership of the idea and, in the end, one of the harshest critics declared that he was optimistic about the initiative.
Both the minister of tourism and the imam were genuinely
enthusiastic. Everyone began to relax as we adjourned for
a dinner downstairs. It was a turnaround from the earlier
confrontational conversation. At that moment, we began
to get to yes.

At dinner, a colleague asked me: "It felt like there were

forty rifles firing at us. How did you dodge all those bullets?" The truth is that I had not tried to dodge any bullets. I had simply sought to respond to rejection with respect, to exclusion with inclusion or, in other words, to *no* with *yes*.

During that meeting, the Abraham Path was born. The West Bank, the place that we had imagined might be the most challenging area for the Abraham Path, would over the following years become the place of greatest local ownership, of most communities involved, and of most travelers walking. Since that opening journey, the Abraham Path has become an established cultural walking trail in a number of countries across the Middle East, receiving thousands of walkers from around the world, and being recognized in *National Geographic Traveller* magazine as the world's best new walking trail. It is still in its early years, but its long-term promise in a region where there is a lot of pain and despair is to build understanding, prosperity, and hope.

It may not be easy to change the dynamic of a difficult interaction or relationship from antagonism and rejection to respect, particularly when you feel under attack, but the rewards are great. By showing respect, we are more likely to receive respect. By accepting, we are more likely to be accepted. By including, we are more likely to be included. If we can say *yes* to the basic dignity of others, getting to yes becomes a lot easier and our relationships at home, at work, and in the world become far more productive and satisfying.

One final challenge remains in the process of getting to yes with yourself: to change the win-lose mindset that so often prevents us from arriving at mutually satisfying solutions.

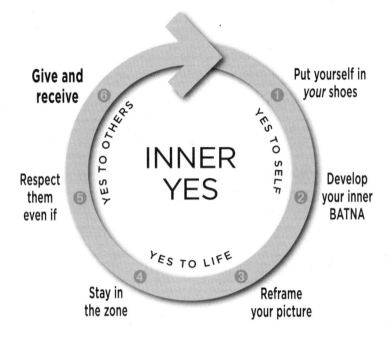

Give and receive
⑥

Put yourself in *your* **shoes**
①

Respect them even if
⑤

Develop your inner BATNA
②

Stay in the zone
④

Reframe your picture
③

YES TO OTHERS
YES TO SELF
YES TO LIFE

INNER YES

GIVE AND RECEIVE

FROM WIN-LOSE TO WIN-WIN-WIN

This is the true joy in life, the being used for a purpose recognized by yourself as a mighty one . . . I am of the opinion that my life belongs to the whole community, and as long as I live it is my privilege to do for it whatever I can.

—GEORGE BERNARD SHAW, *MAN AND SUPERMAN*

As challenging as it can often be to find win-win solutions in our negotiations and relationships, I believe that the process of getting to yes with ourselves allows us—and indeed asks us—to aim for an even more audacious goal. It invites us to pursue "win-win-win" outcomes, victories not just for us and the other side, but also for the larger whole—the family, the workplace, the nation, and even the world. In a divorce, as spouses struggle with each other, how can the needs of the children be met? In a dispute between union and management, how can the organization stay financially healthy to provide good jobs for everyone and their families? In a conflict between two ethnic groups, how will people stay safe?

The key to finding win-win-win solutions that serve everyone is to be able to change the game from *taking* to *giving*. By taking, I mean claiming value only for yourself, whereas by giving I mean creating value for others, not just yourself. If taking is essentially a *no* to others, giving is a *yes*. Giving lies at the heart of cooperation. It is a behavior but it originates inside of us as a basic attitude toward others. Most of us adopt an attitude of giving in certain settings, as when we are with our family, friends, and close colleagues. But how can we cultivate an attitude of giving and cooperation with those who are not so close to us or even with those who may be in conflict with us? That is the challenge.

In many years of teaching win-win negotiation methods, I have watched again and again people learn cooperative negotiation techniques only to revert to win-lose behavior the moment they face a real conflict. In the heat of an argument, when emotions are running high, the fear of scarcity often wins out. We are afraid that, if we cooperate, there will not be enough to meet our needs or the other side will take advantage of us.

It is so tempting, particularly in conflicts, to focus just on claiming value for ourselves rather than creating value for others as well as ourselves. As difficult, however, as others can sometimes be, the opportunity to change the game to win-win-win lies in our hands. We can lead the way by examining and shifting our own attitude.

Whatever the perceived challenges, there are enormous benefits in adopting a basic attitude of giving for our negotiations as well as our lives. In his groundbreaking book *Give and Take,* professor Adam Grant of Wharton Business School presents an impressive array of evidence from academic studies that the most successful people in life, perhaps surprisingly, are "givers," not "takers." It is, of course, important to be intelligent in one's giving and mindful of those who merely take, otherwise you may end up doing yourself a disservice. But the research on the tangible benefits of giving is eye-opening.

One study, for example, carried out by Grant concludes that salespeople who focus on giving genuine service to customers earn more than those who are in it primarily for the money. Another study showed that people who give away more money to charity tend to be happier and end up, on average, earning more. The research suggests that giving works in part because it increases the probability that someone else will do something good for you. Giving, it turns out, is the path to personal satisfaction, both inner and outer.

So how can we strengthen our attitude of giving in our dealings with others? It is worth noting that all the prior steps of getting to yes with yourself lead up to this point. If we feel a sense of satisfaction and sufficiency from within, then it is easier to give to others around us, even when they are difficult. Having addressed our deepest needs, it is easier to address the needs of others. And by *giving* others our respect, we have already, in a sense, adopted an attitude of giving.

Still, the fear of scarcity can be very strong. To cultivate a basic attitude of giving, it helps to root that attitude in our self-interest, in our pleasure, and in our purpose. In other words, give for mutual gain, give for joy and meaning, and give what you are here to give.

GIVE FOR MUTUAL GAIN

The well-known Chinese billionaire Li Ka-Shing, who began his life in arduous and poor circumstances and went on to become one of the wealthiest men in the world, was once asked by a magazine interviewer about the secrets to his business success. One key, he said, was that he always treated his partners fairly and, in fact, gave them a little more than he took for himself. Everyone wanted to be partners with him and it was his partners who helped him to become wealthy.

The first way to strengthen our attitude of giving is to appreciate how creating value for others can help us tangibly meet our needs. Giving need not mean sacrificing our interests. It does not require us to become a Mother Teresa or Mahatma Gandhi. Nor does giving mean giving in to the other person's demands. Giving does not mean losing. Giving in the first instance can simply mean looking for mutual gain, helping others at the same time as we help ourselves. That is the essence of win-win negotiation.

The most successful negotiators I know tend to be people who focus on addressing the interests and needs of their counterparts at the same time as looking after their own needs. In doing so, they find ways to create value and expand the pie for both sides and end up generally with better agreements than people who just try to claim as much as possible for themselves at the expense of others. Solid research supports this approach. In a comprehensive analysis of twenty-eight different studies of negotiation simulations, led by Dutch psychologist Carsten De Dreu, the most successful negotiators turn out to be people who adopt a cooperative approach that focuses on meeting the needs of *both* parties.

In dealing with any conflict or negotiation, we have four possible choices, depending on the concern we show for our interests and the other side's. We can choose a hard adversarial win-lose approach, in which we are concerned about our interests alone. We can choose a soft accommodating approach, in which we show concern only for the other side's interests and not ours. We can choose an avoidance approach in which we don't talk about the issue at all, thereby not showing much concern for either the other person's interests or ours. Or we can choose a win-win approach, in which we show concern for *both* the other person's interests *and* ours.

Much of my work in teaching negotiations and advising parties in conflict has been helping people find their way from an adversarial win-lose approach to a win-win approach. People often learn the hard way by first arriving at an outcome where everyone loses. While an adversarial approach may prove costly and ineffective, a soft accommodating approach typically does not work much better. If we give everything away to please the customers, we may not be in business long enough to serve the customer. If, in taking care of an elderly parent, we wear ourselves out in endless sacrifice, we may burn out and not be available to help at all. Avoidance, the third approach, also has pitfalls: if no one talks about the conflict, it often just gets worse. In the end, creating value for both sides usually produces the best and most sustainable agreements and relationships.

In his book, Adam Grant cites the example of Derek Sorenson, a top-class athlete turned professional negotiator for a leading sports team in charge of negotiating contracts for new players. In one such negotiation, he sat down with the agent of a highly promising young player. Sorenson made a low offer, taking a win-lose approach and acting like a "taker." The agent expressed his frustration repeatedly, pointing out how comparable players were earning significantly higher salaries. But Sorenson would not budge and eventually the agent gave in. Even if it was a loss for the player and the agent, it seemed like a win for Sorenson, saving his team thousands of dollars.

But at home that night, Sorenson had an uneasy feeling. "I could just feel through the conversation that he [the agent] was pretty upset. He brought up a couple points on comparable players, and in the heat of things, I probably wasn't listening too much. He was going away with a bad taste in his mouth." Sorenson recognized the potential toll of his win-lose approach on the relationship as well as on his reputation. So he went back to the agent and met his original request, giving thousands of additional dollars to the player. As Sorenson saw it, he was building goodwill. "The agent was extremely appreciative. When the player came up for free agency, the agent gave me a call. Looking back on it now, I'm really glad I did it. It definitely improved our relationship, and helped out our organization." When we start to appreciate how giving for mutual gain helps us, as Sorenson did, we are motivated as he was to change our attitude from taking to giving.

It also helps that the benefits of giving go well beyond material self-interest.

GIVE FOR PLEASURE AND MEANING

When I teach negotiation, I often use an ancient fable from Aesop. It is the tale of the North Wind and the Sun, who one day started arguing about which one was more powerful. Was the North Wind more powerful or was it the Sun? Unable to resolve the dispute by argument, they decided to put the matter to a test. From on high in the sky, they looked down on the earth and spied a passing shepherd boy. The North Wind and the Sun decided that whoever could pluck the cloak off the shepherd boy's shoulders would be deemed the more powerful one.

So the North Wind went first. He blew and blew and blew as hard as he could, trying to rip off the boy's cloak. But the harder he blew, the more tightly the boy wrapped his cloak around his body and refused to let go. Finally, after a long while, the North Wind took a pause for breath. Then it was the Sun's turn. The Sun just shone, as it does naturally, and bathed the boy in her warmth. The boy loved it and finally said to himself, *What a beautiful day! I think I will lie down for a moment in this grassy meadow and just enjoy the sun.* As he prepared to lie down, he took off his cloak and spread it out as a blanket. So the Sun prevailed in her argument with the North Wind.

I find that this old fable has a lot to teach us about the value of giving. If the North Wind's attitude was to *take,* the Sun's attitude was to *give.* The nature of the Sun is to shine. It does not matter whether a person is rich or poor, kind or mean—the Sun shines on everyone. Its natural approach is win-win-win. And as the fable suggests, the Sun's approach is more powerful and more satisfying than the approach of the North Wind.

To cultivate our attitude of giving, it helps to discover the sheer joy that can come from giving. Much like the sun shines because that is what it does, not because it expects something back, we can discover the pleasure that comes from giving naturally without thinking about receiving a direct or immediate tangible return. Paradoxically perhaps, giving simply for the pleasure of giving can bring us the most satisfaction in the end.

I will never forget a life lesson I learned from a little five-year-old girl named Haley, the granddaughter of good friends, who had fallen gravely ill with leukemia. Lizanne and Gabi, then three years old, went to visit her at Children's Hospital when Gabi was there for one of her innumerable medical appointments. They found Haley in extreme discomfort, her face swollen almost beyond recognition, her hair gone, lying wanly on the bed. Seeing Gabi, Haley turned to her mother and whispered in her ear. Her mother excused herself for a moment, went downstairs to the hospital gift shop, and came back to the room with a large stuffed letter G for Gabi.

It wasn't just Gabi's face that lit up but it was Haley's. She knew, early on, the pleasure of making another child smile. Even in her terrible condition, on the verge of dying, she was able to feel the joy of giving for giving's sake.

When we discover the joy of giving, we give because we feel moved to give. In the first stage of giving, we may give to others simply in order to receive. We may treat the relationship with the other person like a business transaction. In the second stage of giving, however, we give without expecting a direct tangible return.

"My default is to give," says Sherryann, a manager interviewed by Adam Grant who spends many hours a week mentoring junior colleagues at her firm, spearheading a women's leadership initiative, and overseeing a charitable fund-raising project at the firm. "I'm not looking for quid pro quo; I'm looking to make a difference and have an impact, and I focus on the people who can benefit from my help the most."

When we find our motivation for giving in meaning and pleasure, the more we give, the better we feel. And the better we feel, the more we tend to give. Of course, we have to make sure we take care of our needs too, or we will end up feeling used and burned out. There are limits we need to respect, even to giving for pleasure and meaning.

Giving for the pleasure of giving is very different from giving out of obligation. When we feel obliged to give, we rarely feel much pleasure and we often end up feeling unhappy. Consider Scott Harrison's story. Scott had been raised in a household where he was expected to be unselfish and give, but he was never offered a choice. Like many of us, he wore a mask of altruism to gain his parents' and his church community's approval. But in his late teens and twenties, he rebelled against what he saw as hypocrisy and took off his mask. He focused only on pleasing himself with little or no concern for others, making his living promoting nightclubs and fashion events in New York City.

At age twenty-eight, he had all the appearance of success and happiness: lots of money, a Rolex watch, a leased BMW, a girlfriend who worked as a model. Then one New Year's Eve in Punta del Este, Uruguay, where he had rented a huge house, with horses and servants and $1,000 worth of fireworks to blow up in ten minutes, it suddenly hit him.

> I really saw what I had become. Every single thing that I had as a value I had walked away from in this slow burn over ten years. . . . I was emotionally bankrupt, I was spiritually bankrupt, I was morally bankrupt. I looked around me and nobody else was happy either. It was almost as if the veil had been lifted. There would never be enough girls, there would never be enough money, there would never be enough status.

Scott's crisis provoked an intense period of questioning and soul-searching. He asked himself a couple of powerful and disturbing questions: "What would the opposite of my life look like? What if I actually served others?" Having had the experience of false altruism, he was now interested only in the real thing.

After a few months of spending time with himself alone, reading and probing deeply into his own psyche, Scott decided to volunteer as a photojournalist on a medical hospital ship in West Africa, where he served for two years. Moved and inspired by the suffering and courage he had witnessed, he returned home to found an organization called *charity: water*, a charity that raises funds to build wells and provide clean water to hundreds of thousands of impoverished people around the world. Today, his deep need for meaning is being fulfilled. Having spent some time with him, I can attest to his energy and enthusiasm. Describing the joy of watching people drink clean water from the wells he has helped fund, he exclaims, "I am on fire."

Our consumer society has led us to believe that having "things"—material possessions as well as power and success—brings us inner satisfaction. But Scott's story illustrates the truth that, no matter how much we may get, there is never enough. Our neediness can never be satisfied if we meet only our needs.

In contrast, giving that is genuine and freely chosen *can* bring us enduring inner satisfaction, precisely because it meets our deepest need to be useful and connected to others, because it allows us to make a difference in the world of others, and because it just makes us feel good. Paradoxically, it is by giving that we often receive what we most want. When we discover giving for pleasure and meaning, a virtuous circle of giving and receiving begins. But receiving does not become the goal of our giving. We give simply because it is who we are and what we like to do. And by giving in this way, as Scott's story suggests, we create a win not just for ourselves and others, but also for the larger whole.

GIVE WHAT YOU ARE HERE TO GIVE

Perhaps the most enduring way to strengthen our attitude of giving is to find a purpose or activity that makes us a natural giver. Just like a muscle, the attitude of giving benefits from exercise. Through a purpose, giving can become engrained in the fabric of our lives.

A purpose is the answer to the questions *Why* do we get up in the morning? What makes us excited? What inspires us? For some, a purpose may be to raise and care for a family; for others, it might be to play music or create art. For some, it may be to build something that has never been built; for others, it might be to care for a garden. For some, it may be to give service to customers or to mentor younger colleagues; and for still others, it may be to help people who are suffering. If we can discover a purpose that makes us come alive, it can be not only a source of inner satisfaction but also an excuse to give to others around us and to strengthen the giver in us.

Throughout this book, I have shared the story of my daughter's medical challenges. Just as I was concluding the writing, something remarkable happened for her that illustrated the benefits of finding a purpose. One morning, Gabi announced to Lizanne and me that she intended to celebrate her sixteenth birthday, which was four months away, by breaking a Guinness World Record. It had long been a dream of hers and a few years earlier, she had tried for the longest hopscotch course and then for the most socks on one foot. This time she said she wanted to attempt the longest-held abdominal plank, a core-strengthening exercise that involves keeping your body absolutely straight in a horizontal position as you prop yourself up on your forearms and toes.

As I've mentioned earlier, Gabi was born with a medical condition that has required fourteen major surgeries on her spine, her spinal cord, her organs, and her feet in the course of her life. While trying out for the school volleyball team a few months earlier, Gabi's coach had asked her to do the plank while the other girls ran, which Gabi has difficulty doing. The coach was astonished to find Gabi still holding the plank position twelve minutes later when the other girls had returned. Seeing the coach's surprise, Gabi immediately thought, *Whoo, Guinness World Record!* She wrote to Guinness and learned that the official record for women was forty minutes. Gabi then waited two months until after another major surgery to begin her training.

Lizanne and I were surprised, yet not *really* surprised, to find out about Gabi's project. Despite all the adversities in her life, we have never seen her feel sorry for herself. She never falls into the trap of powerless victimhood. We have always marveled at her zest and enthusiasm for life, her ability to take each day and make it fun for herself. We have been astonished at her ability to pick up her life after each surgery, seeing life as essentially on her side. She seems to naturally live in the present, not losing time in regrets about the past or worries about the future. Throughout her childhood, Gabi never lost her underlying *yes* to self and her exuberant *yes* to life.

Lizanne and I were supportive of Gabi's dream and encouraged her to go for it. Weeks went by as Gabi trained to beat the record. In her informal attempts, she went from twenty minutes to twenty-five, to thirty, and once, when her mother was distracting her by asking her questions, she made it past forty minutes. Gabi shared in an interview:

Originally I thought I was going to break the record for me because that's something I always wanted to do. But the idea came up that I could do this for a cause. And I really liked that idea, especially when I figured out that I could do it for Children's Hospital. They helped me not only walk and run, but do something extraordinary. I wanted to help them so other kids like me could have a better experience. I wanted to raise money and awareness so the plank could be something much more than a record.

Gabi's original purpose extended naturally from giving to herself to giving to others as well.

Then, one week before the scheduled attempt, Gabi received an e-mail from the current world record-holder, Eva Bulzomi, alerting Gabi that she had just smashed her own record by an incredible twenty-five minutes. Her new time was 1 hour, 5 minutes, 18 seconds. Guinness had not certified it yet, but it was in process. Lizanne asked Gabi, "Wow, how do you feel about it?"

"This makes it a little harder," Gabi replied in her low-key manner, undaunted and as determined as ever.

Finally the big day arrived. Gabi's friends and family gathered around to watch her make the attempt. After holding the plank position for thirty-five minutes, about halfway toward her goal, she hit a wall of discomfort and pain in her arms and tears began to fall on the mat. Gabi's friends began to sing and entertain her in order to distract her from her pain. As the minutes went by, friends and family started to cheer and to drop down to the floor to do the plank themselves. Finally, at an hour and twenty minutes, Gabi stopped. She had doubled the existing world record. I felt awe and relief as I helped her carefully out of the plank position.

A week later, Gabi appeared on *Good Morning America,* where an official from the Guinness Book of World Records presented her with the official award. The news went around the world on social media as the video of her breaking the record was seen in over a hundred and fifty countries. She not only inspired thousands of people to test their own limits and turn their own perceived weaknesses into strengths, but in the process she raised over fifty-eight thousand dollars for Children's Hospital Colorado, more than eleven times her target.

Gabi was remarkably successful in getting what she wanted and, at the same time, benefiting others, many in ways we will never know. She didn't start her planking project with the purpose of giving to others but she ended there. She learned to appreciate the joy of giving and receiving. As Gabi discovered, nothing strengthens the attitude of giving more than rooting it in a purpose.

Giving what we are here to give, as Gabi's story shows, may be the greatest sustained source of satisfaction life affords us. But when we give from a sense of purpose, it does not need to be grand. I think of my friend Paola, who studied law and became a lawyer. She had a prestigious career but was not happy. Then she remembered that, when she was a child, she used to love to mix hair conditioners and put her lotions on her dog. It seemed random, at first, but it was a clue to what she loved. Mixing hair conditioners for her dog, she used to imagine herself as a chemist mixing potions that would help humanity. So, mustering her courage and using her savings, Paola left the practice of law and set about establishing a business to make natural soaps and help people in that way. This new way of making a living may not have fit her idealized image of a "successful" career, but it brought her happiness because she had found a way to contribute by doing something she genuinely loved.

Our gifts may seem small but often make a significant difference in the lives of others: taking care of a friend's child or of an elderly parent in need, helping a neighbor with a daunting home repair, pitching in at work when a colleague gets sick, or simply offering a gesture of kindness to a stranger in the street. The apparent magnitude of the gift does not matter; what counts is giving in an openhearted way.

Perhaps the greatest obstacle in the way of us giving our gifts is the fear, not of our smallness but of our greatness.

We are afraid not of our limitations but of our talents. The humanistic psychologist Abraham Maslow used the term "Jonah complex" to describe the fear that prevents us from exercising our talents and fulfilling our destiny. The biblical Jonah sought to run away from his fate, which was the call from God to warn the people of the city of Nineveh to leave their violent and wicked ways or be destroyed. Hearing the call, Jonah heads in the exact opposite direction. While crossing the sea on a ship, a great storm threatens the lives of everyone on board. Jonah somehow knows he is responsible and tells the crew to throw him overboard, which immediately brings the storm to an end. Jonah ends up in the belly of a whale and, only after realizing his mistake in resisting his destiny, is released by the whale onto dry land. Jonah travels to Nineveh and carries the warning in time for people to change their ways and be spared the terrible consequences.

This ancient story contains a lot of wisdom: When faced with the opportunity to give our gifts to the world, we often run the other way like Jonah did. We hide our light under a bushel. Only when we face adversity do we wake up and realize that we can only fulfill our purpose if we give what we are here to give, in other words, if we let our light shine for others.

In the course of my work on the Abraham Path, I have had the privilege of studying the ancient stories about Abraham. In the biblical story, Abraham hears the call from God to leave his country and the house of his father and go to a place where he will be shown his true self. In direct contrast to Jonah, Abraham immediately heeds the call and sets off on a journey to follow his destiny. The sages of old used to debate why of all people at the time, only Abraham was selected to receive this call. What made him especially deserving? After much discussion, the sages came to the conclusion that, in truth, *each* human being receives the call. The only difference was that Abraham listened.

Abraham's gift was the simple but powerful lesson of hospitality. As a stranger in a strange land, he received hospitality and he gave hospitality. His tent was said to be open in all four directions to receive guests. The gift that Abraham discovered in himself was to show kindness to strangers. He learned to let his light shine on others. What I have come to appreciate is that perhaps each of us is a bit like Abraham, called to embark on a journey into the unknown. Each of us is given a certain gift that is ours to give, a light within. It is simply up to us to clean the window that looks out and to let our light shine for others.

FROM WIN-LOSE TO WIN-WIN-WIN

I have described earlier in the book the case of my friend and client Abilio Diniz as an example of someone who was trapped in a win-lose fight from which there seemed to be no exit. I would now like to describe how the fight ended.

Throughout the two and a half years of struggle with his former business partner, in which they had sued each other, attacked each other in the press, and blocked each other's initiatives to help their company grow, they had tried to *take* what they wanted from the other—and failed. Neither had succeeded in getting what he really wanted.

When my colleague David and I met with the other side's negotiator, we sought to change the dynamic: instead of presenting the other side with a list of threats, we focused on what each side had the power to *give* the other. Behind all the conflicting positions, Abilio and his partner had two interests in common: freedom and dignity. Each party had the power to offer the other the freedom he wanted to pursue business deals. And each party could offer the other the respect he valued. We proposed that an agreement founded on these two common interests—freedom and dignity—could be a win-win agreement, however difficult that was for the parties to imagine at first.

We discussed how to make such an agreement tangible.

Abilio's partner could release Abilio from a three-year non-compete clause, giving him the freedom he sought to make other business deals. In return, Abilio could agree to leave the board, leaving his partner free to run the company the way he wanted. His partner could exchange Abilio's voting shares for nonvoting shares that Abilio would then be free to sell in the stock market. Both parties could release a joint press statement wishing the other well. And so on. In short, the game could shift from win-lose to win-win.

There were many difficulties and legal complexities, of course, but this simple change in the dynamic from taking to giving made all the difference. In four intense days, the parties were able to get to yes and put a final end to this bitter business battle. Abilio gave a gracious farewell talk to the company's executives and another to all the employees in which he spoke respectfully of his former partner and wished all of them well. His partner offered Abilio a valuable athletic training organization, belonging to the company, which had been a real passion for Abilio.

What was truly astonishing to all concerned was the degree of satisfaction expressed afterward by both Abilio and his partner, hitherto archenemies. It was not a barely acceptable compromise that each grudgingly agreed to, but a solution that left each feeling remarkably satisfied and relieved with the outcome.

Starting the negotiations by focusing on what they could *give* each other, rather than what they could *take* resulted in a genuine win-win outcome. In fact, it went well beyond a win-win to a win-win-win solution as the benefits spread far and wide beyond the two parties to their families, to the company and its hundred and fifty thousand employees, and even to the society at large.

It was not an easy process for Abilio. Like most of us, he began as his worthiest opponent. But he worked hard to turn himself into an ally. With a strong tendency to react by attacking, he tried his best to go to the balcony, even if not always successfully. While he judged himself harshly at times, he also made great efforts, with the help of others, to put himself in his own shoes and uncover his true needs. While occasionally he blamed the other side, he always remembered in the end that he alone was responsible for his life.

At times Abilio fell prey to the fear of scarcity, but then he reframed his picture of life and remembered his power to make his own happiness. Whenever he got trapped in the past, he was able to come back to the present moment to see what could be done. A real fighter, he took an antagonistic stance, but he remembered when it was important to offer respect to his adversary. The last obstacle for Abilio to overcome was the win-lose mindset, which he did by changing his attitude from taking to giving.

Like just about everyone, Abilio was imperfect in the process of getting to yes with himself, but his disciplined efforts to get out of his own way were sufficient for him to succeed in getting to a big yes he wanted with the other side. "I got my life back," he told me. "These are the best times in my life."

Each one of the six steps helps us to transform the win-lose mindset into a win-win-win mindset. The crowning move is to shift our basic underlying attitude toward others from taking to giving. At first we may give in order to receive, then we learn to give without receiving a direct return, and finally we learn to give in fulfillment of our purpose. By changing our basic default mode to giving, not only can we get to yes with ourselves, experiencing inner satisfaction, but we will also find it easier to get to yes with others, achieving outer success. Thus begins a circle of giving and receiving that has no end.

THE THREE WINS

I imagine yes is the only living thing.

—E. E. CUMMINGS

This book began with a question that is a universal human dilemma: How can we get what we truly want while satisfying the needs and concerns of others in our lives—family members, work colleagues, clients, and others?

The core premise of this book is that *the better we are able to get to yes with ourselves, the better we will be able to get to yes with others.* Perhaps no factor has a greater impact on our relationships and negotiations than our underlying attitude toward ourselves, toward life, and toward others.

The most powerful change we can make in our life is to change that inner attitude from *no* to *yes.*

Very little in life may be under our full control, but the choice between yes and no is ours to make at any moment. We can choose to say yes or no to *ourselves,* to be either our best ally or our worst opponent. We can choose to say yes or no to *life,* to treat life either as friend or foe. We can choose to say yes or no to *others,* to relate to them either as possible partners or implacable adversaries. And our choices make all the difference.

Getting to yes with yourself makes possible three kinds of wins—a win within, a win with others, and a win for the whole.

A WIN WITHIN

In the morning when I look at myself in the mirror, I like to remind myself that I am seeing the person who is probably going to give me the most trouble that day, the opponent who will be the biggest obstacle to me getting what I truly want. I find it valuable to review in my mind, even if for a few minutes, the six steps of the inner yes method in order to prepare myself for any challenges that may arise that day. I like to ask myself questions for each step. This process helps me get out of my own way—and I hope it can help you too:

1. **Put Yourself in *Your* Shoes.** Can you notice the inner critic at work—and simply observe your thoughts and feelings without judging? What underlying needs do your feelings point to? What do you *really* need?

2. **Develop Your Inner BATNA.** Are you blaming anyone or anything for your needs not being met? What benefit does this blame provide you—and what are the costs? Can you commit to take care of your deepest needs no matter what?

3. **Reframe Your Picture.** Do you feel like life is in some way against you? How can you make your own happiness today? If life is challenging, can you nonetheless choose to say yes to it, just the way it is?

4. **Stay in the Zone.** Are you carrying any resentments about the past or anxieties about the future? What will it take to let go and accept life as it is today? What is one small step you can take to stay in the zone, where you are at your best?

5. **Respect Them Even If.** Are you feeling any antagonism toward anyone? What is it like to be in their shoes?

Even if they are not showing you respect, can you still respect *them*?

6. **Give and Receive.** Do you feel a fear of scarcity in any situation you are currently facing? What will it take for you to change the game from taking to giving, from win-lose to win-win-win?

Each step addresses a particular obstacle that gets in the way of us getting what we most want in life. Each step makes the next step easier to take. Even if they may sound simple, none of these steps is easy, particularly in the daily conflicts we all face. Indeed, the work of arriving at an inner yes is some of the hardest work anyone can do, all the more so because it is invisible.

As valuable as the method can be, it will be of little use without continual practice. Understanding the six steps can help you a lot, but in the end, no one can do the work but you. As with any sport, while you may never be perfect at it, you will gradually get better and better. I like to think of each step as being like a muscle; the more I exercise it, the stronger it gets. As powerful as each muscle is alone, exercising all six together is what allows you to move toward your desired destination.

How you actually go through the process of getting to

yes with yourself is particular to you. You will have your favorite ways to go to the balcony, for example. Some like to go for a solitary walk in the park, others to go out for a coffee with a good friend who can listen. I encourage you to adapt this method to your own needs. Make it your own so that it works best for you.

I have found that this journey from *no* to *yes* with myself is not a single trip, but ultimately a lifelong journey. I have been on this journey for a long time and expect to be on it for as long as I live. There is always more for me to learn. One truth keeps getting clearer for me: there is no bigger yes than the yes inside, no bigger win than the win within. An inner yes brings a growing sense of calm and contentment and a deepening feeling of satisfaction and sufficiency. If that were the only win, it would be enough, but there is more.

A WIN WITH OTHERS

The next win is a win with others—our colleagues and customers, our spouses and children, and even our negotiating opponents. Once we have gotten to yes with ourselves, it is considerably easier to get to yes with others, as difficult as that sometimes can be. As we have seen, each of the six steps provides us with a missing prerequisite for success in negotiation. Putting yourself in *your* shoes helps you put yourself in the other person's shoes. Developing your inner BATNA helps you develop your outer BATNA. Reframing your picture of life helps you reframe your relationship with others—and so on. The key work in negotiation starts from within.

It is all too tempting to react in the middle of a difficult conversation or tough negotiation. If you have the luxury of preparing before a problematic conversation or negotiation, you can run through the six steps in advance to bring your best ally instead of your worst opponent to the conversation or negotiation table. If you are on the fly, you will still be able to rely on the inner yes method if you have steadily practiced it over time. Even in the midst of conflict, you can stay on the balcony, calm and collected.

I have found, moreover, that the process of getting to yes with yourself not only makes it easier to *resolve* conflicts, but also actually helps *prevent* conflicts from arising in the first place. By not reacting, by staying calm and grounded, you will avoid being provoked and will be less likely to take attacks personally. You are far less likely to say or do things that you will later come to regret. With an attitude of sincere respect and a genuine willingness to help address the needs of others, you will be able to resolve matters long before they escalate into serious disputes. You will get along naturally with others with a minimum of conflict.

A WIN FOR THE WHOLE

Three decades ago, when I had the privilege of working with Roger Fisher on writing *Getting to Yes,* our goal was to help people shift from adversarial approaches to cooperative methods for dealing with differences at work, at home, and in the community. But our dream was bigger than that. It was to help the world take a step toward peace. We were concerned about humanity itself, whose fate in an age of mass destruction ultimately rests on our abilities to resolve disputes in a cooperative fashion.

Although our world today is filled with scarcity, inequity, and violent strife, the truth is that, thanks to the technology revolution, there is enough to meet everyone's needs. We know how to end hunger, how to prevent war, and how to use clean energy to save the environment. The central obstacle in the way is us. It is our difficulty in coming together to cooperate. In order to build a better, safer, and healthier world for ourselves and for our children, we must be able to deal with our differences constructively and creatively. Getting to yes may be highly challenging, of course, but, having worked on some of the world's most difficult conflicts, I am convinced that it is fully possible. And the first radical step in the process is for us to get to yes with ourselves.

Getting to yes with ourselves brings a larger and more generous perspective that benefits everyone around us and makes possible not only a win with others, but a third win for the larger whole. The work on ourselves inspires us to imagine and to work toward a world in which every single human being matters.

Perhaps no one has illustrated this possibility better in recent times than Nelson Mandela. In prison for twenty-seven years, Mandela went to the balcony and began to observe and listen to himself: "Learn to know yourself . . . to search realistically and regularly the processes of your own mind and feelings" was the lesson he drew.

Mandela avoided falling into the blame game and took full responsibility for his life, his needs, and his relationships with his enemies. He boldly reframed the picture, choosing to see life on his side, despite all evidence to the contrary. He let go of old resentments and grievances, forgiving his enemies.

When Mandela emerged from prison, he brought with him an extraordinary spirit of respect and inclusion, welcoming people of all races in the new South Africa he envisioned. Drawing on his own inner satisfaction, he gave unstintingly of himself to others. The result was that he was able to lead his nation to a win-win-win agreement aimed to benefit all by ending the evil of apartheid and ushering in a new democratic era for South Africa.

Fortunately, most of us will not face the magnitude of the challenges that Mandela faced, but we can nonetheless take inspiration from him and make use of the same basic principles in our daily lives. Choosing to say yes to ourselves, to life, and to others, we can change the fundamental game we play from win-lose to win-win-win. And therein lies hope for us, for our families, for our workplaces, and for humanity.

I have devoted much of my professional life to trying to prevent and stop wars. Peace is my passion. If someone had told me thirty-five years ago that the key to peace was inner peace, I would have thought them utopian and unrealistic. I preferred instead to work on something more practical— which was to focus on strategies for negotiation. Now I have come to realize that I was the one who was perhaps unrealistic in believing that we could arrive at a sustained peace in this world without also doing the necessary work within ourselves.

WINNING THE GAME OF LIFE

My great hope is that getting to yes with yourself will not only improve your ability to negotiate effectively with others, but more broadly will help you create the inner satisfaction that will, in turn, make your life better and your relationships healthier. I hope that changing your inner attitude from *no* to *yes* will help you win the most important game of all, the game of life.

No matter how great the challenge can be at times, the potential rewards are far greater: peace of mind and heart that can help you bring peace in the family, peace in the workplace, and peace in the larger world.

I wish you much success . . . and much peace!

ACKNOWLEDGMENTS

This book began with a single reader—myself—as I started to jot down notes seven years ago to help learn how to get to yes with myself more effectively. It was a deeply personal project as, faced with challenges in my life and in the lives of those around me, I felt compelled to look more deeply inside myself. As a fan of frameworks, I began to develop a simple framework to help myself remember. Only later on, when I showed my evolving notes to family and friends did I think it might be of use to others as well.

With encouragement from friends, the process became much easier. I would like to offer warm thanks to Curt Manfred Mueller, who believed in this book long before it was written, to David Friedman and Robert Gass, who gave me early insightful feedback and enthusiastic support on many walks, to David Baum, Francisco Diez, Patrick Finerty, Mark Gerzon, Margo King, David Lax, Jamil Mahuad, Ronald Mueller, Simon Sinek, Gary Slutkin, and John Steiner, whose encouraging comments helped me persevere, and to Donna Zerner, who offered extensive editing advice on an early draft.

Finding the right stories to convey the message is never easy. For their instructive and inspiring stories, I would like to thank Robert Chapman, Judith Ansara Gass, Adam Grant, Scott Harrison, Azim Khamisa, Jamil Mahuad, Paola Mahuad, Jill Bolte Taylor, Gabi Ury, Lizanne Ury, Dennis Williams, and Jerry White. I am especially indebted to Abilio Diniz for his friendship and generosity in allowing me to use the example of his successful conflict resolution in this book.

I could not have been more fortunate in finding an agent who understood and supported my project in every way. Jim Levine guided the evolution of the manuscript, found a good publishing home for it, and gave valuable counsel throughout the process. He has been a true friend and I am extremely grateful to him as well as to his colleagues and family.

Then there was the talented team at HarperOne. My editor, Genoveva Llosa, has been a sheer pleasure to work with as she thoughtfully reviewed the manuscript and offered many savvy editing suggestions to tighten the logic and the language. To her and all her capable colleagues, including Mark Tauber, Claudia Boutote, Kim Dayman, Melinda Mullin, Gideon Weil, Miles Doyle, Michele Wetherbee, Dwight Been, Terri Leonard, Natalie Blachere, Laurie McGee, Carol Kleinhubert, and Hannah Rivera, I offer my immense thanks.

Writing became easier because of the able assistance

in running my office and protecting my time. I benefited greatly from the dedicated and highly skilled support of Cathy Chen-Ortega and her predecessors Essrea Cherin and Myka McLaughlin, to whom I am very grateful indeed. For a writing refuge in nature, I would like to express my special thanks to the fine people of Aspen Winds—Dot, Phil, Sharon, and Ryan.

As the book evolved, the challenge loomed of how to build a solid bridge between the interior world of self that I was exploring and the exterior world of negotiation. In this process of bridge building, I was fortunate to be able to try out the draft manuscript on a variety of readers who were kind enough to give me their thoughtful feedback. I would like to thank Goldie Alfasi, David Baum, Barry Berkman, Shelby Boyer, Todd Brantley, Helena Brantley, Sara Davidson, Francisco Diez, Renée DuPree, Lindsay Edgecombe, Patrick Finerty, Norman Galinsky, Mark Gerzon, Bill Gladstone, Daniel Greenberg, Margo King, Joan Levine, Joshua Levine, Jamil Mahuad, Kiana Moradi, Leopoldo Orozco, Shana Parker, Julissa Reynoso, Stephanie Rostan, Raphael Sagalyn, Monica Sharma, John Siffert, David Sikes, Lindsey Moses Sikes, Roberta Sotomaior, Kerry Sparks, John Steiner, Danielle Svetcov, Elizabeth Ury, Monika Verma, Lauren Wasserman, Joshua Weiss, John Wilcockson, and Tim Wojcik.

This book, in the end, is the fruit of what I have learned from my experience and my teachers. It is to my teachers that I would like to dedicate this book. When I was in my teens, the writings of Friedrich Nietzsche, Ralph Waldo Emerson, and Henry David Thoreau deeply inspired me with their philosophy of saying yes to life, come what may. I learned from my close study of the words and life of Mohandas K. Gandhi how essential inner work is to outer action. In my twenties, Roger Fisher enthusiastically introduced me to the field of negotiation, generously taught me about mediation, teaching, and writing, and inspired me to make this my life's work. I am forever indebted to him as well as to my aunt Aline Gray and my friend Frank Fisher for introducing me to Roger.

Ever since high school I have been a passionate reader of philosophy and wisdom from Plato to Lao-Tzu to Ramana Maharshi, but in recent years I have had the benefit of experiencing such wisdom firsthand from my friend Prem Baba. For his clear, insightful, and compassionate lessons, I am profoundly grateful.

My biggest debt is to my wife, Lizanne, whose love and support sustained me throughout. She listened with deep care and encouragement to each of many drafts. From Lizanne, I have learned priceless lessons about gratitude, presence, and all matters of the heart. She and our children—Chris, Thomas, and Gabi—are my greatest blessings.

NOTES

Introduction

p. 4, **"If you could kick . . ."** This quote comes from the online source BrainyQuote.com. See http://www.brainyquote.com/quotes/quotes/t /theodorero120663.html.

Chapter One: Put Yourself in *Your* Shoes

p. 16, **The *Financial Times* called the dispute** "Brazil's Billionaire Baker Who Came of Age in Captivity," *Financial Times,* July 1, 2011.

p. 23, **a mother's account of witnessing** The author is Charlotte Z. Rotterdam in *Fearless Nest: Our Children as Our Greatest Teachers.* Edited by Shana Stanberry Parker (http://www.lulu.com, 2010), 93. For more information, see http://www.fearlessnest.com.

p. 25, **"To observe without evaluating . . ."** I heard this quote by Jiddu Krishnamurti from my friend Marshall Rosenberg. I also found it at The European Graduate School, http://www.egs.edu/library /jiddu-krishnamurti/biography/.

p. 27, **Psychologists have estimated** "Stop Fighting Your Negative Thoughts," *Psychology Today,* May 7, 2013, http://www.psychology today.com/blog/shyness-is-nice/201305/stop-fighting-your-negative -thoughts. Also, from the University of Southern California's Laboratory of Neuro Imaging, see http://www.loni.usc.edu/about_loni /education/brain_trivia.php.

p. 27, **"If you talked to your friends . . ."** This saying I heard from David Baum. Variants can be found at http://behappy.me/OneToughMother

Runner/if-you-talked-to-your-friends-the-way-you-talk-to-your-body
-youd-have-no-friends-left-21380 and at http://www.experienceproject
.com/question-answer/If-Someone-In-Your-Life-Talked-To-You-The
-Way-You-Talk-To-Your-Self-Sometimes-How-Long-Would-They-Be
-There/452083.

p. 30, **"Sadness . . . was not well received . . ."** Joanna Barsh, *Centered Leadership: Leading with Purpose, Clarity, and Impact* (New York: Crown Business, 2014), 236–37.

p. 32, **"In the old story . . ."** This story of the Holy Grail has many variants. I owe this one to Elias Amidon.

p. 39, **As Carl Rogers . . . once noted** Carl Rogers, *On Becoming a Person: A Therapist's View of Psychotherapy* (New York: Mariner Books, 1995), 17.

Chapter Two: Develop Your Inner BATNA

p. 43, **the Tylenol crisis in 1982** A more detailed version of the Tylenol story can be found in an article by N. R. Kleinfield, "Tylenol's Rapid Comeback," *New York Times,* September 17, 1983.

p. 48, **"I didn't like that image . . ."** Jerry White, *I Will Not Be Broken: 5 Steps to Overcoming a Life Crisis* (New York: St. Martin's Press, 2008), 58.

p. 51, **In his insightful book** David Schnarch, *The Passionate Marriage: Keeping Love and Intimacy Alive in Committed Relationships* (New York: Henry Holt, 1997), 124. The original pseudonyms used by Schnarch are Bill and Joan.

p. 57, **"I'm no longer willing . . ."** Schnarch, *Passionate Marriage*, 124.

Chapter Three: Reframe Your Picture

p. 65, **"This," Einstein declared** Robert D. Dilts, *Strategies of Genius: Volume II* (California: Meta Publications, 1994), 20–21.

p. 70, **"A human being," Einstein once wrote** Walter Sullivan, "The Einstein Papers: The Man of Many Parts," *New York Times,* March

29, 1972. This article also can be found reprinted here: http://news .google.com/newspapers?nid=1964&dat=19720329&id=sYMyAAAAI BAJ&sjid=x7cFAAAAIBAJ&pg=6595,5077091.

p. 72, **"Our left brain . . ."** "Does Our Planet Need a Stroke of Insight?" January 3, 2013, http://www.huffingtonpost.com/dr-jill-bolte-taylor /neuroscience_b_2404554.html. For a more in-depth discussion, see Jill Bolte Taylor, *My Stroke of Insight: A Brain Scientist's Personal Journey* (New York: Plume, 2009).

p. 77, **"How then can we reframe . . ."** I would like to acknowledge my debt to Stephen Covey and Lynne Twist for their thinking about the shift from the scarcity mindset to the abundance or sufficiency mindset. For an in-depth exploration, see Stephen Covey, *The 7 Habits of Highly Effective People: Powerful Lessons in Personal Change* (New York: Free Press, 1989) and Lynne Twist, *The Soul of Money: Transforming Your Relationship with Money and Life* (New York: W. W. Norton, 2003).

p. 78, **"The lesson . . . ," Gilbert says** Daniel Gilbert's TED talk, "The Surprising Science of Happiness," https://www.ted.com/talks/dan _gilbert_asks_why_are_we_happy. For more analysis, see Daniel Gilbert, *Stumbling on Happiness* (New York: Knopf, 2006).

p. 78, **"From the time I was young, . . ."** This is from an interview conducted by Petria Chaves and Fabiola Cidral on the radio show "Caminhos Alternativos," December 1, 2013.

p. 83, **"We've discovered scientific proof . . ."** "Pay It Forward," last modified June 1, 2007, Dr. Robert Emmons's article on gratitude, http:// greatergood.berkeley.edu/article/item/pay_it_forward. For more in-depth discussion, see Robert Emmons, *Thanks!: How Practicing Gratitude Can Make You Happier* (New York: Mariner Books, 2008).

p. 85, **By absolute safety, Wittgenstein meant** Ludwig von Wittgenstein, "A Lecture on Ethics," 1929, reprinted on http://www.geocities .jp/mickindex/wittgenstein/witt_lec_et_en.html.

p. 85, **Dr. Viktor Frankl tells the story** Viktor E. Frankl, *Man's Search for Meaning* (Boston: Beacon Press, 2006), Kindle edition.

Chapter Four: Stay in the Zone

p. 94, **Research psychologist Mihaly** Mihaly Csikszentmihalyi, *Flow: The Psychology of Optimal Experience* (New York: Harper Perennial Modern Classics, 2008).

p. 95, **"It's a very strange feeling. . . ."** This quote from Mark Richardson comes from Jeff Grout and Sarah Perrin, *Mind Games: Inspirational Lessons from the World's Finest Sport Stars* (New York: Capstone/Wiley, 2006).

p. 100, **"Tell me the truth . . ."** "Mandela Beat Apartheid 'Demon': Clinton," July 18, 2013, http://www.news24.com/SouthAfrica/News/Mandela-beat-apartheid-demon-Clinton-20130718.

p. 101, **"We cannot live . . ."** "Christo Brand & Vusumzi Mcongo (South Africa)," March 29, 2010, http://theforgivenessproject.com/stories/christo-brand-vusumzi-mcongo-south-africa/.

p. 102, **"If you live, you will make mistakes . . ."** "Laugh and Dare to Love," originally published in 1995, interview with Maya Angelou, http://www.context.org/iclib/ic43/angelou/.

p. 104, **"My life has been full . . ."** I found this quote at BrainyQuote.com. See http://www.brainyquote.com/quotes/quotes/m/micheldemo108601.html.

p. 107, **My friend Judith** Rotterdam, *Fearless Nest*, 102–3. For more information about Judith, see Judith's website http://www.sacredunion.com.

Chapter Five: Respect Them Even If

p. 115, **The atmosphere was tense.** This example comes from a personal conversation with Dennis Williams, June 2014.

p. 119, **While I was writing this book** These interviews were done under the auspices of the Harvard-NUPI-Trinity Syria Research Project and compiled into a report entitled "Obstacles to a Resolution of the Syrian Conflict," by David Lesch with Frida Nome, George Saghir, William Ury, and Matthew Waldman, September 2013.

p. 121, **"If we could read the secret . . ."** This quote comes from Henry Wadsworth Longfellow, *The Prose Works of Henry Wadsworth Longfellow: Outre Mer and Driftwood* (Boston: Houghton Mifflin, 1886).

p. 124, **"The increased compassion . . ."** David DeSteno, "Gray Matter: The Morality of Meditation," *New York Times Sunday Review*, July 5, 2013, http://www.nytimes.com/2013/07/07/opinion/sunday /the-morality-of-meditation.html?hp.

p. 125, **Larry married a Mexican American woman** "A Teacher, a Student, and a 39-Year-Long Lesson in Forgiveness," by Tom Hallman Jr., at http://www.oregonlive.com/living/index.ssf/2012/04/a_teacher_a _student_and_a_39-y.html.

p. 129, **Lincoln paused and addressed** Clifton Fadiman (gen. ed.), *The Little Brown Book of Anecdotes* (Boston: Little Brown, 1985), 360.

p. 132, **"When I got the phone call . . ."** "Azim Khamisa & Ples Felix (USA)," March 29, 2010, http://theforgivenessproject.com/stories /azim-khamisa-ples-felix-usa/.

p. 140, **Since that opening journey** "Ten of the Best New Trails: Discover the Best New Hikes from Wales & New Zealand to the Balkans and the Middle East" by Ben Lerwill, *National Geographic Traveller (UK Edition)*, April 2014, 72–73.

Chapter Six: Give and Receive

p. 145, **The research suggests that giving** Adam Grant, *Give and Take: A Revolutionary Approach to Success* (New York: Viking, 2013), 7.

p. 147, **Everyone wanted to be partners** "Thoughts of Li Ka-Shing," December 29, 2006, http://www.forbes.com/2006/12/29/li-ka-shing -biz-cx_tf_vk_1229qanda.html.

p. 147, **In a comprehensive analysis** Carsten K. W. De Dreu, Laurie R. Weingart, and Seungwoo Kwon, "Influence of Social Motives on Integrative Negotiation: A Meta-Analytic Review and Test of Two Theories," *Journal of Personality and Social Psychology* 78 (2000): 889–905. Cited in Grant, *Give and Take*, 213.

p. 149, **"I could just feel . . ."** Grant, *Give and Take,* 250–54.

p. 152, **"My default is to give"** Grant, *Give and Take,* 22.

p. 154, **"I really saw . . ."** Scott Harrison's story, http://www.charitywater .org/about/scotts_story.php.

p. 158, **"Originally I thought . . ."** Gabi Ury's website, http://www .gabiury.com.

p. 160, **The news went around the world** The source for this piece of information is Steve Priola, who made the video.

p. 162, **The humanistic psychologist** Abraham H. Maslow, *The Farther Reaches of Human Nature* (New York: Penguin, 1993).

Conclusion

p. 176, **"Learn to know yourself . . ."** Anthony Sampson, *Mandela: The Authorized Biography* (New York: Vintage Books, 2012), Kindle edition, chapter 17.

ABOUT THE AUTHOR

William Ury, cofounder of the Harvard Negotiation Project, is one of the world's best-known experts on negotiation. He is the coauthor of *Getting to Yes,* an international bestseller with over thirteen million copies in print, and author of seven other books including *Getting Past No* and *The Power of a Positive No.*

For the past thirty-five years, Ury has served as a negotiation adviser and mediator in conflicts ranging from boardroom battles to coal mine strikes to wars in the Middle East, Latin America, and the Caucasus. He has taught negotiation and mediation to tens of thousands of leaders in business, government, and civil society around the world.

Ury is founder of the Abraham Path Initiative, which seeks to inspire understanding, prosperity, and hope by opening a long-distance walking trail across the Middle East retracing the journey of Abraham and his family. Trained as a social anthropologist, with a B.A. from Yale and a Ph.D. from Harvard, he lives with his family in Colorado.

For further information, please visit www.williamury .com or send an e-mail to info@williamury.com.